KUNGL. VITTERHETS HISTORIE OCH
ANTIKVITETS AKADEMIENS

HANDLINGAR

ÅTTIOSJUNDE DELEN

KUNGL. VITTERHETS HISTORIE OCH
ANTIKVITETS AKADEMIENS HAND-
LINGAR UTGIVAS MED ANSLAG UR
HUMANISTISKA FONDEN

KUNGL. VITTERHETS HISTORIE OCH ANTIKVITETS
AKADEMIENS HANDLINGAR, DEL 87

THE HISTORIC ORIGIN
OF THE EIGHT HOURS DAY

STUDIES IN ENGLISH TRADITIONALISM

BY

GÖSTA LANGENFELT

GREENWOOD PRESS, PUBLISHERS
WESTPORT, CONNECTICUT

Library of Congress Cataloging in Publication Data

Langenfelt, Gösta, 1888–
    The historic origin of the eight hours day; studies
in English traditionalism.

    Reprint of the 1954 ed. distributed by Almqvist &
Wiksell, Stockholm, which was issued as del 87 of
Kungl. Vitterhets-, historie- och antikvitetsaka-
demiens handlingar.
    1. Eight-hour movement--History. 2. Alfred the
Great, King of England, 849-901. I. Title.
II. Series: Vitterhets-, historie- och antikvitetsaka-
demien, Stockholm. Handlingar, del 87.
HD5166.L35   331.2'572   73-19224
ISBN 0-8371-7314-0

ARBETET TRYCKT MED ANSLAG
UR HUMANISTISKA FONDEN

Originally distributed in 1954 by Almqvist & Wiksell, Stockholm

Reprinted with the permission of the Royal Swedish Academy
of Letters, History, and Antiquities

Reprinted in 1974 by Greenwood Press,
a division of Williamhouse-Regency Inc.

Library of Congress Catalog Card Number 73-19224

ISBN 0-8371-7314-0

Printed in the United States of America

PREFACE

Labour's demand for eight working hours a day was first voiced in 1831 by Robert Owen and in 1833 by his Society for National Regeneration. Already in 1817, however, in a letter to the London press, Owen had suggested that grown-up workers should not work more than eight hours a day.

There existed at that time, just as it does now, a tradition that Alfred the Great of Wessex (d. 900) had divided the 24 hours of the day and night into 3 portions: 8 hours for work, 8 hours for recreation, and 8 hours for prayers (later altered: diversion). This tradition had been repeated in chronicles and historical works right down to 1850, and is sometimes still repeated. The aim of this present work is to prove that there is an unmistakable connection between Labour's demand and the Alfredian tradition.

It might be added that there are no traces of a threefold division of the 24 hours of the day in any other country. Hours of a definite length belong to a period when it is possible to measure the time of the day and night accurately by means of a reliable time-measurer. Consequently Primitive Man, as well as advanced civilizations: Mesopotamia, India, China, Persia, Greece, and Rome, were unable carefully to divide the day into such definite portions. The wheel-clock would seem to be the necessary instrument for such a division. It is also characteristic that there are no traces of such a division in the literary remains of those civilizations, or otherwise, as is ascribed to Alfred the Great.

Alfred the Great lived long before the invention, and the introduction, of the balance-clock, it is true, but according to contemporary testimony he invented a time-measurer founded on the same principle of time as that of the inventor(s) of the wheel-clock. Other influences cannot, then, be traced in the moulding of the idea of a threefold division of the 24 hours. The Alfredian tradition is first mentioned by

William of Malmesbury (ab. 1123) and has continued to live down to our own days.

To assume that British labour leaders would have hit upon a similar idea that eight hours' daily work is enough for a human being must to a critical mind seem absurd, since this supposition demands a fresh and independently formed idea of identical kind. And this at a time when the Alfredian tradition of the division of the day was rather well-known. The startling fact that in no other country in Europe or America the eight hours' working day has been discussed, or practised, before Owen, and — what is more — that works in other languages: Latin, French, Spanish, German, speaking of this ideal amount of daily work, always, even in ages gone by, acknowledge its English origin, should warn those who seem to think that it "just happened" — without any historical background. By saying that the Alfredian tradition gave the impetus to Labour's demand for an eight hours' day, the preposterous conclusion that there existed an eight hours' day in Alfred's days, is naturally not drawn, — for obvious reasons.

The present investigation examines notions of time in primitive societies; time-measuring instruments in Classical Antiquity; monastic rules; etc. The long series of mentions of the Alfredian tradition from William of Malmesbury through every century, even every decade, down to 1850 is minutely reported. But it was thought necessary also to give the social background of every epoch of English history. The law texts quoted refer, however, primarily to the working-time of labourers and workmen, and their leisure, through the centuries. Wherever literary writings give a clue to the length of the working-time, they have been quoted too. Scholars, except Prof. Thorold Rogers and the advocates for an 8 hours' day in the 1890's, agree on the whole on the question of working-time in pre-industrial periods. Concerning the working hours in industrial undertakings, especially in the textile ones, after 1800, *all* investigators: political economists, historians, technicians, etc., are of one accord that the extension of working hours, also of the children's, was scandalous. This is also borne out by the findings of contemporary government committees. Thus, it was thought not to be necessary to mention *all* the writers on working conditions in mid-industrialism. Mr. and Mrs. Hammond's work *The Town Labourer 1760—1832* and Dr. M. W. Thomas's book *The Early Factory Legislation* are of paramount value and have frequently been quoted.

Lastly, the full list of English chroniclers and historians might serve as a useful index for investigators.

The Swedish "Humanistiska Fonden" has granted 3.600 Swedish kronor for the publication of this work.

In 1937 I also had financial support for studies in English libraries from the following Swedish trade unions: Fångvårdspersonalens förbund, Svenska Elektriska Arbetareförbundet, Svenska Gruvindustriarbetareförbundet, Svenska Handelsarbetareförbundet, Svenska Metallindustriarbetareförbundet, Svenska Pappersindustriarbetareförbundet, Svenska Polisförbundet, Svenska Sinnessjukvårdspersonalens förbund, Svenska Sko- och Läderindustriarbetareförbundet, Svenska Skorstensfejeriarbetareförbundet, Svenska Sågverksindustriarbetareförbundet, Svenska Textilarbetareförbundet, Svenska Transportarbetareförbundet, Telegraf- och Telefonmannaförbundet, and Socialdemokratiska föreningen in Ystad.

I am very grateful to Dennis E. Rhodes, of the British Museum, London, and Vincent Petti, B. A. Lond., for supplying me with references to, and relevant passages in, not easily accessible works, to Edward Carney, B. A. Lond., for revising my English, and to John Haycraft, B. A. Oxon., for proof-reading.

I.

Primitive man had no accurate means of measuring time by dividing the day, as we do, into a fixed number of absolute units. He was naturally aware of the difference between day and night, but he was quite incapable of expressing with any accuracy the duration of an action or the point of time at which something had been or was to be done. In practice, however, a system of comparative values grew up in most communities which provided a rough standard of time measurement. This rule of thumb method is amply illustrated by Prof. M. P:son Nilsson in his Primitive Time Reckoning (p. 42). The position of the sun, the moon, and the stars was, of course, a means of defining time anywhere, in any tribe, but especially in tropical countries. *Sun* was sometimes used for *day*. It was even possible to indicate the future by pointing to the sun, saying, "I will be here to-morrow when the sun is there". The Waporogo in East Africa hold one arm vertically raised: that is 12 o'clock noon, and the other hours (or time-units) are indicated by varying angles formed by the arm from the body. Similar systems are naturally found abundantly in tropical countries where the sunshine is intense. Also the length of the shadow can serve the purpose. Even in Ancient Greece the shadow gave a clue to time, as in *Aristophanes*, Ekkles. 652: "when the staff is ten feet, to go perfumed to dinner". Meals (for instance, sanskrit *abhipitvam*, evening, from *pitus*, meal-time); domestic work (milking-time, etc.); tending animals (for instance, the time for the cattle to drink; Irish *im-buarach*, morning, "at the yoking of the oxen"), became chronological terms. In Madagascar the duration of half an hour is expressed by the word "rice-cooking", while a moment is described as "the frying of a locust"; the Cross River natives express the passing of less than a quarter of an hour by saying "the time in which maize is not quite roasted"; Malays, Javanese, and Achinese use "a blink of the eyes" in its literal sense (whereas Germ. *Augenblick*; Engl.

the twinkling of an eye: James, The Kingis Quair str. 163: *in twink-lyng of ane eye*; Swed. *ögonblick*, have extended in time). In New Britain "the smouldering of a torch" represents the time between sunset and sunrise.[1] Similar terms are used to express a short duration of time in the English language of the Middle Ages. In William Langland's The Vision of Piers Plowman, which was written about 1377, we find at line 348 (B text), the phrase "in a pater noster while", that is, the action took just as long as it did to read a pater noster; and likewise in one of the Paston Letters (78, 1448) we read "And all thys was don, as men sey, in a Pater Noster wyle". Similar expressions in English were (quoting NED) *speche whyle* (1430); *miserere whyle* (1450); *breathing-while* (1593); *pissing while* (1553), later turned by Wycherley, the comedy writer, into a *making water while* (1676). The sense of the word *while* may be extended into a *life while* (1300), i. e. a lifetime. Other expressions are *breathing-fit* (1589); *breathing-space* (1650); *breathing-time* (1599); "'twixt owl-light and the dark" (Taylor 165, 1622), "in the squeezing of a lemon" (Goldsmith, She stoops to conquer, p. 335); *mile*, as a vague measure of time: the time in which one might journey a mile (1330 →); hence *mile way* (13 ... →) = 20 minutes; *furlong* a short distance ($^1/_8$ mile); hence the time taken in walking this (1384 →); a *furlong way* = 2 $^1/_2$ minutes; Chaucer, Canterbury Tales, E 1 l. 516: "Soone after this, a furlong wey or two, He prively hath toold al his entente". 1 *league* was equal to 3 miles, but was very seldom used in English texts. *League* (see below p. 39), used in a Latin document from York, 1352, must be the same as 3 miles: half a league = $^1/_2$ hour. Otherwise breakfast had to be reduced to 10 minutes (= $^1/_2$ mile), which is obviously not possible.

All these Middle and Early Modern English expressions referred to a space of time, but there were also terms for a point of time. In the Gesta Romanorum, a 15th c. collection of short prose tales, there is the story of "Plebeius the Emperoure" (No. xxv), in which a knight tells

---

[1] EDM. ANDREWS, A History of Scientific English, New York, 1947, p. 108, states that to the Tahitians "the hours of the day are marked by the 12- to 18-inch sun tide, as accurately as on any chronometer". An 18th c. native *aratai*, pilot, told Captain James Cook when he was setting up an observatory to study a transit of Venus, that his chronometer was wrong because the white man could not predict the rising of one constellation after another as he could. Neglect of this advice nearly made the astronomers miss the eclipse.

his wife, who is besieged by three lovers, to "sey to the fyrst knyght, þat he bryng his mony *at mydnyte*; and to the seconde, þat he bryng his mony *at þe thirde cokkis crow*; and to the third knyght, þat he bryng his mony *in the morowe*". (My italics.) While the first and the last expressions are still current to-day, the second is rather too vague for modern people, at least for town-dwellers. In his diary Pepys writes, 24 Sept. 1667, "we stayed till past candle-light"; 26 Aug. 1668, (was) "there till after candle-lighting". Similar vague expressions are still more or less used in current speech: at *daybreak, day-peep, day-rawe, day-red, day-rim, day-spring, daylight-gate, dawn, sunrise,*[2] *in the (early) morning, at noon, in the afternoon, evening, at sunset, dark, after dark* (it droȝe to þe derke; 1400—50), *until dusk* (1893), *after dusk* (1720), *at nightfall, night, midnight, in the small hours* (all from NED).[3]

Mechanical means of measuring time were in use at an early stage of civilization. The Greek *clepsydra*, or water clock, introduced in Rome in the middle of the 2nd c. B. C., was an earthenware bowl containing water, which "stole away" (hence its name) through a hole, or holes, bored in the bottom of the bowl. But the clepsydra was not exactly a precision instrument, since the trouble was that it gained about fifteen minutes every hour. The use of the clepsydra is reflected in the Latin expressions *aquam dare*, to give the advocate speaking time, *aquam perdere*, to waste time. Another device, probably Babylonian, was the sun-dial, which had been perfected through the centuries and was eventually used to solve intricate geometrical problems. The sun-dial, with which we are still familiar, divided the day from sunrise to sunset into twelve equal parts; the night was also supposed to have a similar division into twelve parts or *horas*. Even in Mediterranean countries, the relative length of day and night varied considerably between summer and winter, though not so markedly as in more northerly climates. Consequently the length of an hour varied according to the period of

---

[2] Cf. CHAUCER, Canterbury Tales A 2 p. 28: at the sonne up-riste. — But in those days the balance clock was also used, for cf. ibid. B 2, p. 154: For by my chilindre it is pryme of day.

[3] Sketches by Boz, ch. 7, p. 33 (Baudry, Paris 1839): he displayed a most extraordinary partiality for sitting up till three or four o'clock in the morning; FORSTER, Life of Dickens. 1872 I, p. 129: The smallest hour was sounding from St. Paul's into the night before we started. — Thus the small hours after the small numbers.

daylight. The equal parts of the day were called *temporary* or *planetary* hours. The practical complexities of this method of time-keeping are quite beyond the grasp of the disciplined clock-watcher of modern times, but it may be supposed that the Romans clung to the old system of counting only sunrise, midday, and sunset. Abu'l Hassan, an Arab, who lived about the beginning of the 13th c., was, however, able to reform the sun-dial, so that every 24th of *the day and night* was measured and became equal in length, or an *equinoctial* hour. But historians do not know whether this became common knowledge. In the interval between the twelfth and the sixteenth centuries the balance clock was invented, and our modern hour, one 24th of the day and night, began to be used in reckoning time, although it was long before the old way of calculating the hours of the day was abandoned.

The Anglo-Saxons in England were well aware of the problems of time-reckoning and realized the value of a division of the day and night into 24 equal parts. Their knowledge of astronomy came to them chiefly through Latin treatises by way of the Church: it was considered part of a priest's duties to be able to reckon time. The Venerable Bede, a Jarrow monk and the author of the Ecclesiastical History of the English Nation (d. 735), wrote several books on time and time-reckoning (ed. by Charles W. Jones: Opera de Temporibus. Cambridge. Mass. 1943). In his De Tempore Ratione (p. 182) Bede tells us that time may be computed in three ways: a) in the natural way, b) according to habit, c) according to authority. He goes on to speak (ch. III) of the minor divisions of time, considering the hour as a twenty-fourth part of the day and night; in ch. V he distinguishes between the vulgar way of regarding the time between sunrise and sunset as a day, and the correct method of applying the word day to the whole period of 24 hours; in ch. VII the night is defined as the dark period of the 24 hours.[4] Then, in ch. xxxi, he shows that day and night differ in

---

[4] BEDE also says that the night is instituted for the repose of the body (De Tempore Ratione ch. vii, p. 194). Similarly AELFRIC, De Temporibus Anni, p. 18: The night is set for people to rest in this world. — It is surprising that as late as 1066 the period of 24 hours is called *night* in English, although one has to translate it as *day*. Survivals of this use of the word *night* for the whole 24 hours are found in the terms *fortnight* (14 nights) and *sennight* (7 nights), meaning respectively 14 and 7 days. See LIEBERMANN, Die Gesetze der Angelsachsen, II, 2 595. For the reason of using *night*, see NILSSON loc. cit. p. 13 ff. — An interesting use of the word *day* is

length in different places, such as at Meroe (in Egypt), in different
parts in India, in Alexandria, Italy, Britain, and in the Thule of
Pythias, largely basing his argument on various Latin Classics, especially Pliny. About Thule he gives the old story by Pliny that it has
six months' day in summer and six months' night in winter. — Thule
is situated 6 days' sailing northwards from Britain. Once, in his Ecclesiastical History (Bk I, ch. i) Bede mentions the summer nights of
Britain, "And because it (Britain) lies almost under the very north pole
of the world, it has bright nights in summer, so that often at midnight
it is a matter of doubt to the beholders whether the evening twilight
still lingers or the first dawn of morning has already arrived, since
the sun during the night goes not far beneath the earth on its return
to the east through the regions of the north: whence also it has days
of great length in summer, and, on the contrary, nights of great length
in winter, that is, of eighteen hours' length, by reason of the sun then
departing into the regions of the south. It has very short nights in
summer, and very short days in winter, that is, of only six equinoctial
hours; whereas in Armenia, Macedonia, and Italy, and other regions
of the same latitude, the longest day or night is fifteen hours, the
shortest full nine."[5] As can be seen, Bede's astronomy suffers from the

---

found in Anglo-Saxon Wills, ed. by DOROTHY WHITELOCK, Cambridge Univ. Pr. 1930,
p. 48: tw(egra) manna dæg ealswa þa foreword sprecað = for two lives as the terms
state; p. 68: er daye 7 after daye = both before my death and after. Perhaps the
sense is better rendered: before (my) lifetime (birth?) and after (my) lifetime (death)?

[5] Bede's account is surprising. The monks of the Benedictine order to which Bede
belonged went to bed shortly after sunset. They would therefore be familiar with
the long northern twilight when daylight lingers on long after sunset — a pheno-
menon quite different from the sudden nightfall of Mediterranean countries. From
my own experience, midnight is quite dark in Yorkshire during the summer months
(Civil evening twilight at 21.27 in York, 54°, on July 4) — which seems to contradict Bede's statement, — though I have found it light enough at Inverness on July 4
to read a newspaper with ease after 10 p.m. — which struck me as curious. (Sunset
at Inverness, 57 1/2°, at 21.04; civil twilight at 22.16, on July 4.) It is evident that
Inverness is farther to the north than Bede's Jarrow and York, but taking the
different latitudes in consideration it seems improbable that midnight in summer
at Jarrow could be as light as Bede makes it. Plummer (ed. 1896) refers (II 7) to
Venerabilis Bedae Opera (ed. Giles, 1843, 1844; viii. 255. 256), where Bede speaks
of the midnight sun in Thule, in northernmost Britain, and in Scythia. AELFRIC's
De Temporibus Anni (ed. H. Henel, EETS orig. s. 213. 1942), said to have been
written in 993 (Henel p. xlv), contains also this passage (ibid. 50): "On ðam ylcan

defects of medieval scholarship, though it was of much practical value to his contemporaries. Bede also gives information (De Temporibus Liber p. 295) about the moments and hours: 4 points, 10 minutes — these, of which ten in an hour, have no historical connection with the modern minute, = one sixtieth of an hour, as in The Vision of Piers Plowman, B text, 1377: *minute while* (NED), — and 11 moments; the day (repeating the vulgar notion of the day as being only between sunrise and sunset, but more correctly 24 hours); (p. 297) about solstices and equinoxes, etc. Aelfric (?955—?1006) follows Bede in his De Temporibus Anni, but has borrowed from other sources (ib. p. liv). We cannot detail all the information he gives, but point out a few distinctions in measuring time: a *prica* = one fourth or one fifth of an hour; that is what Bede calls *points* (Recepit autem hora IV punctos ... et in quibusdam computis V punctos. Bede); he also renders Bede's "viii partes unius horae" by "a little more than half an hour". (A Latin

---

earde norðeweardan beoð leohte nihta on sumera swilce hit ealle niht dagige swa swa we sylfe foroft gesawon." (In the north of this same country there are bright nights in summer so that it is as if it were dawn all night, which we have very often seen ourselves.) Henel supposes then Aelfric to have been born in the north of England and to have come to Winchester as a youth (see p. xlv et seq.), and that Aelfric refers to "the brightness of midsummer nights (which) is certainly much more remarkable in the north of England than in the south". But there is no hint that Aelfric refers to *midsummer* nights, and as to their brightness in the north of England, see my argument above. AELFRIC may possibly have remembered Bede's words in the Ecclesiastical History and interpolated them here, since De Temporibus Anni abounds with loans from several sources, but otherwise mainly follows Bede's books in time-reckoning. (Cf. also Review of English Studies, July 1944, p. 233). Pliny's theories may also have contributed to both Bede's and Aelfric's statements in this respect: calculating thus, that if Thule is only six days distant from Britain and if it enjoys daylight both day and night in summer, north England ought to share in some of this Thulean brightness in summer. There is also a chance that the Benedictine Bede considered the time when the monks rose from sleep at the end of the eighth hour to be about midnight (see p. 14 below), i. e. about 2 or 2.30 a.m.; then the dawn in northern England has begun, and though "yond light is not day-light", it is fairly bright. Not only Pliny speaks of the length of the summer days in Thule, but Procopius also mentions the midnight sun in Thule. It was over the horizon for 40 days and nights, which is more reasonable than Pliny's statement. half a year. See PROCOPIUS, The Gothic War, transl. by H. Dewing (n.d.). TACITUS, Agricola, ch. 12, mentions early sunrise in northern Britain, and in Germania, ch. 45, he says that in the Arctic Sea, north of the Swedes, the light of the setting sun lingers on until next sunrise.

source has it: Recipit autem hora IV punctos, X minutes, XV partes).
And (p. 10) he says expressly: "We call one day from sunrise to
evening, but in books it is said that one day is from sunrise to next
sunrise (from the rising of the sun till he comes back to where he rose
earlier); and in that space are counted twenty-four hours". Aelfric's
term is *tid*, which meant hour, as for instance (p. 42), "Feower 7
twentig tida beoð agane þæt is an dæg 7 an niht". Another Anglo-
Saxon *rimcræftig preost*, a priest skilled in time-reckoning, was Byrhtferth. In his Manual, written in 1011 (ed. S. J. Crawford, EETS orig.
s. 177, 1929), Byrhtferth also says that the word *day* should properly
be used for the 24 hours of a day and night (p. 6), and (p. 112) he
says, "The word day is used in two ways — *naturaliter et uulgariter*,
i. e. in a natural and a popular. It is the nature of a day to have 24
hours from the rising of the sun until it shows its light again on high.
Vulgaris uel artificialis dies, that is to say the vulgar or artificial day,
is from the rising of the sun until it sets and returns to the joy of mankind. The day which has 24 hours has also 96 points ...". In Byrhtferth's division of the *day* (p. 118) there are no less than fourteen
different units: atoms, moments, points, minutes, hours, quadrans,
days ..., but we see already here that Byrhtferth is not consistent, or
logical, since he divided the day itself into days, and even months.
It is clear that by *day* he means time. The important thing, however,
is that, like the other OE computists, he distinguishes between the
natural day of 24 hours of equal length, and the artificial day between
sunrise and sunset. In England during the Middle Ages it was necessary
to stress this difference. Geoffrey Chaucer (d. 1400) writes in his Canterbury Tales (The Squire's Tale, 1.108): "in the space of o day
natureel, (This is to seyn, in foure and twenty houres)", meaning the
period between one sunrise and the next. John de Trevisa, the English
chronicler, points out in 1398, "Some daye is artyfycyall and some
naturell ... a naturell daye conteynyth xxiiii houres" — here 'artificial' refers to the old way of reckoning twelve hours between sunrise
and sunset. Even Eden, the well-read geographer, in his Arte Nauiga-
tionis (1561) thinks fit to explain, "The houre naturall or equall, is a
.24. parte of the day naturall ... The artificiall or temperall houre, is
a twelfth parte of the daye arcke or the nyght arcke." (NED).

❈   ❈

❈

St. Benedict of Nursia (d. ab. 544), the founder of the Benedictine monastic order, prescribed a rule for his monks, in which "the horarium is set out ... with a fullness and simplicity that leaves nothing, save the addition of clock hours, to be desired" (Dom David Knowles, The Monastic Order in England, Cambridge 1940. p. 639), but Prof. Knowles also observes that (p. 4, footn. 2) "The silence of the Rule together with absence of clock-time and the variations introduced for seasonal or liturgical reasons make complete accuracy (in carrying out the horarium) unattainable". How the completed horarium worked in practice is explained by Cuthbert Butler, himself a Benedictine (Benedictine Monachism, London 1919. pp. 275—88). He shows how the system would work out in terms of Roman time-reckoning: "The day, i. e. the period from sunrise to sunset, was divided into twelve equal 'horae', and likewise the night, or period from sunset to sunrise, into twelve equal 'horae'." Consequently, only at the vernal and the autumn equinox were the 'horae' of the day and those of the night of equal length (= 60 minutes); in summer the day-hours were longer than the night-hours, in winter vice versa. Besides, sunrise and sunset depended on the geographical situation of the monasteries. In Rome, near Monte Cassino, on the longest day of fifteen natural hours the artificial hour (since there were only twelve) would amount to 75 modern minutes. The shortest day in Rome is 9 natural hours, so the twelve artificial hours lasted only 45 minutes each. On November 1st in Rome the sun sets at 4.45 p.m. and rises at 6.30 a.m. This means that the night contains 13 $\frac{3}{4}$ natural hours and so an artificial hour is 69 minutes. Butler's calculations, though too involved to be given here in full, are essential to an understanding of the Benedictine horarium, which is thought by some scholars to have played a part when Alfred the Great, King of England (d. 900) — or, preferably, the Alfredian tradition, first mentioned by William of Malmesbury (about 1123), — divided the 24 hours of the day into three parts of 8 hours each. According to Butler, St. Benedict uses in other contexts the expressions *tertia plena*, *decima plena*, to signify the completion of the hour; cf. also "usque in horam secundam plenam lectioni vacent: hora secunda agetur tertia", i. e. 'they are to read until the completion of the second hour', and then, 'at two the office of tierce is to be said', 'two' being two natural hours after sunrise, about 7 o'cl. at midsummer, when the sun rises et 4.30 and the artificial day-hours are of 75 minutes (Butler p. 277 f.). This way of reckoning hours is said to conform to Roman practice, for which The Cambridge Companion to Latin Studies is referred to. Cf. also Anders Gagnér, Zur römischen Zeitrechnung (Strena Philologica Upsaliensis, Uppsala 1922), p. 212 ff., p. 223 (conclusion). Now St. Benedict told his monks to rise at *the eighth hour*, by which he meant the end of the eighth hour. The monks had to go to bed half an hour after sunset — which is at 5.15 p.m. on Nov. 1st, and at 5 p.m. at Christmas.

The first night-hour	4.45—5.54 p.m.
” second ” ”	5.54—7.3 p.m.

. . . .

The eighth night-hour	12.48—1.57 a.m.

The end of the eighth hour was therefore about 2 a.m., though it varied, of course, from season to season, since the night-hours were sometimes 75 minutes, sometimes 69 minutes, and sometimes 53 minutes. However one can say that (the end of) the eighth hour occurred roughly between 2 and 2.30 a.m. This implies that in winter the monks slept $8\,^3/_4$ to $9\,^1/_2$ modern hours every night. During the winter season the time allotted for various tasks was usually (ibid. p. 280 f.):

	Hours	
office in church	4	
'meditatio'	$1\,^1/_2$	
reading	$3\,^3/_4$	
manual work	$5\,^1/_4$	
sleep, meals	$9\,^1/_2$	24 hours

The same at the vernal equinox, March 7th:

office in church	3	
reading	4	
manual, or other, work	$6\,^1/_2$	
'meditatio'	1	
sleep, meals	$9\,^1/_2$	24 hours

On an ordinary summer's day:

office in church	$3\,^1/_2$	
reading and 'meditatio'	$3\,^1/_4$	
manual, or other, work	8	
sleep (in the night $6\,^3/_4$, in the day $1\,^1/_2$), meals	$9\,^1/_4$	24 hours

The Benedictine monks did manual labour, though not a great deal, by working in the fields during two periods of the (summer) day: one stretch early in the morning and another from 2 p.m. to 5 or 6 p.m. To-day the Italian peasants have a different system — they begin work at daybreak and continue until about 10 a.m., when they leave the fields because it is too hot to work any longer. They return to the fields after their siesta at about 4 p.m. and work as long as there is daylight enough. In St. Benedict's time labourers usually went to bed at sunset and since the first recruits for his monastery were mostly Italian labourers, it was natural that this custom should find its way into the horarium. Besides, in days when candles were expensive, most people went to bed shortly after sunset.

The influence of the Benedictine rule in Anglo-Saxon England was considerable. The first Christian missionary to England, the Abbot Augustine, was a Benedictine; the Venerable Bede (d. 735) was also a Benedictine; William of Malmesbury (d. 1143) was yet another. The first monastery in Southern England, at Dorovernum, was Benedictine, and by 1010 the Benedictine rule prevailed all over England (Liebermann loc. cit. II: 2, 305). There exists an OE translation of St. Benedict's rule (EETS orig. s. 90; see ch. vii, x, xi, xli, xlviii); and several ME versions (EETS orig. s. 120). It is not necessary to discuss their treatment of the regulations, since they are identical, or nearly identical, with the Latin original. There is no indication in the Benedictine rule, or in the daily routine becoming habitual in the English Benedictine monasteries, of a threefold division of the 24 hours of the day. Neither is there any in the Cistercian rule, as we shall presently see.

St. Bernard (of Clairvaux) was born in 1090, the son of a nobleman. At the monastery of Citeaux, which was founded by Robert, a Benedictine reformer, in 1098, he became a monk in 1111. But already in 1115 St. Bernard and a number of his fellow-monks had laid the foundation of another reform monastery at Clairvaux, where St. Bernard became the abbot. The object of the reformers was to revive the field-work of the monks, which had been the aim of St. Benedict, and, before him, of St. Augustine (354—430) in his work De Opere Monachorum (ab. 400). The emphasis given to manual labour, and especially to work in the fields, in the monastic rule of the Bernardines brought about a division of their daily occupations into three different parts, in a manner very like St. Benedict's original plan: liturgical prayer, private reading (for which private prayer could at all times be substituted), and regular labour. The labour varied according to the seasons: "in the winter it formed a single spell of some four hours between Chapter (which followed Mass and Terce) and dinner, in the summer the single period was split into two, the earlier and longer taking place after Chapter (which followed Prime) and lasting some two hours". (Knowles 639). The first Cistercian monastery in England was founded without official recognition at Tulket in 1123, but the reputation of St. Bernard's rule had spread over the Continent and Britain long before that date.[6] Henry I of England (see Knowles 175) favoured the Bernardines and founded several monasteries of that order in England: at Waverley, Surrey, in 1128—9, and at Rievaulx (Yks) in 1131—2. Since the rules of St. Benedict and St. Bernard were observed to the letter by the two monastic orders, the monks continued to use the old system of time-reckoning. Even after the invention of the balance-clock they kept to their old horarium, and only in 1429 did the Cistercians switch over to natural hours.[7]

It is clear then that William of Malmesbury, the first chronicler to mention (or the originator of) the Alfredian tradition of a threefold division of the 24 hours of the day, did not find in the rules of St. Benedict and St. Bernard any tradition of such a division, assigning 8 hours for work, 8 hours for prayer and 8 hours for sleep. The actual horarium forbade this. Prof. Knowles writes to me (Sept. 2, 1948): "I do not think William of Malmesbury got the threefold division from Cistercian customs. They nowhere mention it. The monastic threefold division is always of the *waking* life — into prayer, reading & work. Nor do I think that they would have explicitly allowed as much as 8 hours to sleep."

According to Bilfinger [Die antiken Stundenangaben (1888), Die mittelalterlichen Horen und die modernen Stunden (1892), and Der bürgerliche Tag (1888)], as well as other authorities, there is no men-

---

[6] Since St. Bernard and William of Malmesbury were born in the same year (1090) it seems unlikely that the former's rule should have influenced the latter.

[7] See BILFINGER, Die mittelalterlichen Horen und die modernen Stunden. 1892, p. 161. — The time-table of a modern Trappist monastery, given a fictional name, but really La Trappe de Notre-Dame-d'Igny, is described by the French writer J.-K. HYUSMANS in his book En Route (ed. Plon, Paris 1918, p. 233 et seq.); but he mentions no allocation of eight hours of the day to manual work.

tion of a division of the 24 hours into three such periods, much less any prescription or rule. From the Early Middle Ages we have the Salernitan distich, *Sex horae somni satis est pueroque senique: / Da septem pigro nulli concesseris octo*, that is, "Six hours sleep is enough for boys and old men. Give seven to the lazy man, (but) do not admit to anybody eight (hours)." Fynes Moryson, An Itinerary containing his ten yeeres travell through ... Germany ... Italy ... (1616, ed. 1908 in Glasgow, III 453) records another prescription, "The Italians say, / Cinque hore dorme un' viandante, / Sette un' studiante, nove ogni furfante. / A Traveller five howers doth crave / For sleepe, a Student seven will have, / And nine sleepes every idle knave." Another, probably Salernitan, hexameter is: "Sept(em) horas dormire sat(is) est juvenique senique", that is, "To sleep seven hours is enough for youths and old men." A modern version, which probably is related to both, runs: "Six hours' sleep for a man, seven hours' sleep for a woman, eight hours' sleep for a fool." But these verses do not explain William of Malmesbury's threefold division of the day.

II.

Pre-eminent among Old English rulers and statesmen was Alfred of Wessex (849—?900). His success in war freed his kingdom from the Danish yoke, and his political insight and statesmanship made Wessex supreme among the English kingdoms — a supremacy which foreshadowed the eventual unity of England. But it is not only as a successful politician that Alfred claims his pre-eminence: he was equally devoted to the task of educating and civilizing his people. In his Preface to the West Saxon version of Gregory's Pastoral Care he deplores the state of ignorance into which the English nation had fallen. Even priests no longer know Latin — the key to all the knowledge and culture of the Middle Ages. Alfred revived the teaching of Latin, but, still more important, he made a number of Latin works available in the vernacular. These were books which reflected his fervent Christianity: Boethius on the Consolations of Philosophy; the Ecclesiastical History of England by the Venerable Bede; and the World History of Orosius, a Spaniard; the Dialogues and Pastoral Care of Gregory; and the Psalter. The prestige which Alfred's work gave to the West Saxon dialect of Old English was so great that it became the literary language of England until the Conquest and even later. Much of the work of translation was done by Alfred himself and he contributed prefaces to the translations and added passages of his own composition to the History of Orosius. His concern that these translations in the vernacular should be disseminated as widely as possible is shown by his instructions that a copy of the Pastoral Care should be sent to every diocese.

The Anglo-Saxon Chronicle, though it is said to have been begun by Alfred, does not give much information about him, and for many years of his reign the entries are sporadic, It is quite by chance that we know so much of him. In 883, a Welsh priest called Asser was persuaded by Alfred to come to his court to help him with his educational projects. Later, Asser was made a bishop, and, full of enthusiasm for the work of his royal patron, he began to write his Life of Alfred. This work, which was probably influenced by Einhard's Life of Charlemagne, is said to have been finished by 893. Although Asser's Life seems to have existed in several copies, none of them have survived. One MS was published by Archbishop Parker in 1574, but the original was subsequently destroyed in the early 18th c., and so Parker's edition is all that remains to us. The value of Parker's work is impaired by his mismanagement of the text, for he interpolated parts of another MS, the Annals of St. Neot, into Asser's work. The discovery that Parker's edition was inaccurate led many scholars to doubt the existence of an authentic Life of Alfred. Later editors, Wise in 1732 and Petrie (Hardy) in 1848, were careful to distinguish by brackets what they considered spurious. A careful analysis of the text was published in 1904 by W. H. Stevenson (Asser's Life of King Alfred), who is convinced that the bulk of Parker's edition comes from a document contemporary with Alfred. If we allow this account as evidence of Alfred's life and work, the range of his achievement becomes even wider.

Alfred's technical resourcefulness is shown in the account of his naval strategy against the Danes, to be found in the Chronicle for the year 897. He is credited with the invention of a new type of warship: "næron nāwðer ne on Fresisc ჳescæpene ne on Denisc buton swā him selfum þūhte þæt hie nyt(t)wyrðoste beon meahten". A more remarkable invention is ascribed to Alfred by Asser who credits him with the invention of an accurate way of measuring time. (Stevenson edn 89). Asser says that Alfred had promised to devote half his bodily and mental faculties, day and night, to the service of God. Asser's biography continues: "But because he could not distinguish with any exactitude the hours of night owing to the darkness and the hours of daylight owing to the heavy rains and thick fogs, he began to consider by what certain method he could, without any uncertainty, keep faithfully unto death the promise (to serve God) which he had given."

"After having thought about this for some time he found eventually a wise and useful method: he ordered his chaplains to bring a sufficient quantity of wax, brought together in penny-weights, and had them weighed on a two-pounds balance; and when so much wax had been measured as weighed 72 pennyweights, he then asked the chaplains to make six candles, each of equal weight, so that every candle had 12 inches marked on them along their length. When he had thus discovered this way, the candles burned for 24 hours, faultlessly, day and night, in front of the holy relics of many of the chosen ones of Our Lord, which always accompanied him everywhere. But since they could not burn during the whole of one day and night, they being lighted at the vesper of the preceding day, because of a severe draught sometimes stirring day and night without stopping through the doors and the windows of the churches, through the mortar and the *tabularum*, or through the many rifts of the walls and the thin tents, which forced them to burn down earlier than they ought to have done and before the exact hour, by ending their light. He then thought how he could prevent such a draught; and when he had found a way, both ingenious and wise, he had a lantern constructed of wood and ox-horn. For white oxhorn split into thin layers by axes does not shine (be transparent) less than glass vessels. This lantern was made, as was said before, in a beautiful way of wood and horn, and when, at night, a candle was put in it, it burned brightly, inwards and outwards, without being hindered by a breath of air, because he had similarly had a door of horn made to the opening of the lantern. This invention finished, the six candles burned, one after the other, for 24 hours without interruption, neither quicker nor slower. When they had burned down, others were lighted."[8]

---

[8] 103. 11. Sed quia distantiam nocturnarum horarum omnino propter tenebras, et diurnarum propter densitatem saepissime pluviarum et nubium aequaliter dignoscere non poterat, excogitare coepit, qua ratione fixa et sine ulla haesitatione hunc pro-

There are several points of interest in this account of Alfred's invention. The candles weighed twelve pennyweights each, or, according to Stevenson (p. 381) $^5/_8$ oz. avoirdupois, that is 17 grammes, and they were each 12 inches in length, that is, nearly 30 centimetres. A candle made to these specifications would be rather tall and very slender. In order to find out whether such a candle could be made I asked the Liljeholmen's Stearinfabrik (Stockholm) to make one according to Alfred's specification as it is given by Asser. Eighteen grammes of beeswax were used in making the candle and it was provided with a very simple wick; when made, it weighed 18 grammes and measured 12 inches exactly and burnt for 4 hours and 20 minutes — the extra twenty minutes are accounted for by the extra gramme. Alfred's calculations were therefore correct, and six candles would burn for 24 hours.

The only fault with this candle was that it indicated the right time only at every inch-notch, which was every twenty minutes. On the

----

missum voti sui tenorem leto tenus incommutabiliter, Dei fretus misericordia, conservare posset.

(104). His aliquandiu excogitatis, tandem, invento utili et discreto consilio, suos capellanos ceram offerre sufficienter imperavit, quam adductam ad denarios pensari in bilibri praecepit; cumque tanta cera mensurata fuisset, quae septuaginta duos denarios pensaret, sex candelas, unamquamque aequa lance, inde capellanos facere iussit, ut unaquaeque candela duodecim uncias pollicis in se signatas in longitudine haberet. Itaque hac reperta ratione, sex illae candelae per viginti quatuor horas die nocteque sine defectu coram sanctis multorum electorum Dei relinquiis, quae semper eum ubique comitabantur, ardentes lucescebant. Sed cum aliquando per diem integrum et noctem ad eandem illam horam, qua anteriori vespera accensae fuerant, candelae ardendo lucescere non poterant, nimirum ventorum violentia inflante, quae aliquando per ecclesiarum ostia et fenestrarum, maceriarum quoque atque tabularum, vel frequentes parietum rimulas, nec non et tentoriorum tenuitates, die noctuque sine intermissione flabat, exardescere citius plus debito ante eandem horam finiendo cursum suum cogebantur, excogitavit, unde talem ventorum sufflationem prohibere potuisset, consilioque artificiose atque sapienter invento, laternam ex lignis et bovinis cornibus pulcherrime construere imperavit. Bovina namque cornua alba ac in una tenuiter dolabris erasa non minus vitreo vasculo elucent. Quae itaque laterna mirabiliter ex lignis et cornibus, ut ante diximus, facta noctuque candela in eam missa, exterius et interius tam lucida ardebat, nullis ventorum flaminibus impedita, quia valvam ad ostium illius laternae ex cornibus idem fieri imperaverat. Hoc itaque machinamento ita facto, sex candelae, unaquaeque post alteram, per viginti quatuor horas sine intermissione nihil citius, nihil tardius lucescebant. Quibus extinctis, aliae incendebantur. (STEVENSON p. 89.)

other hand, this coincides with the *mile-way*. A league, comprising
three mile-ways, was an hour. Alfred could only measure half an hour
by reckoning an inch and a half. When 3, 6, 9, and 12 inches respectively had burnt, Alfred knew that 1, 2, 3, and 4 hours had passed.
It is clear that only one candle burnt at a time, and not all six at once,
for Asser definitely says that "the six candles burnt one after another",
and that "at night *a* candle was put in it", i. e. the lantern. The first
candle was lit at vesper, which was therefore the starting-point of
Alfred's horologium. It is obvious from the text that this time measurer
travelled with Alfred to many places in the country, for partly this
is said, partly it is implied by mentioning *church* and *tent* in the plural
and the precise description of many different sorts of walls, crannies
and draughts.

Asser's account deals with a day of 24 natural hours and he does
not regard day and night as two independent units of twelve artificial
hours each. It is clear from the very nature of Alfred's invention that
he wanted to follow the natural 24 hour day, since the candles could
not be used to measure a variable hour. In fact, Alfred has "the credit
of anticipating by several centuries the use of this, the modern, system,
which is so largely the result of the introduction of the wheel-clock.
(Stevenson p. 339).[9] The later tradition of three eight-hour periods is
not mentioned by Asser; it can only be traced back to William of
Malmesbury. But the four-hour candle would be quite convenient for
measuring such a division. Eight-hour candles would have been too
cumbersome for the lantern. Two four-hour candles would be just as
suitable for the purpose.

In Anglo-Saxon England and everywhere else in Christendom the
working classes were tied to the soil by law and custom; their hours
of labour were long and their duration was wholly at the discretion
of the overlord. What little information we have about working hours
is chiefly drawn from the Anglo Saxon laws where the living condi-

[9] It is remarkable that BILFINGER (Die mittelalterlichen Horen ...) does not
mention Alfred's horologium.

tions of the working classes occasionally come within the scope of ecclesiastical, criminal or civil law.

Workmen were either free, half-free, or slaves; they were almost all field-workers, since there were no town industries in the modern sense. Even the "free" men were bound by certain obligations and were not wholly free. The human rights of the workers were overlooked by the governing class: in fact, they had no rights, they were more or less chattels. Serfdom was an acknowledged fact, and the lowest class of society was recruited every year by prisoners of war, people in debt, and children who were born or sold into slavery. These last are mentioned in Thorpe's ed. of Ancient Laws (p. 21): "Though someone sells his daughter into servitude, let her not be altogether such a *theowa* as other females are." — a pious wish but difficult to carry out. The caste system is shown in laws which allowed that slaves could be killed with impunity; they were whipped in cases when a free man would pay a fine; they were not entitled to holidays, except for the Monday, Tuesday and Wednesday before Michaelmas; and though they were Christians, they could be sold to heathens. They had no regular holidays, except for the common weekly holiday of Sunday. This was a Christian principle, enforced more especially because a Sunday free from work was part of the teaching of the Christian missionaries. Already in Wihtraed's laws (695—6) § 9 we find: "If on his lord's request a day servant (*esne*) performs slave-work on Saturday after sunset until Monday morning, the lord must pay a fine of 80 shillings."[10] *Sunset* was, then, the dividing point even on Saturdays, not *none* nor midday. The freeman would also be fined for working on Sundays, "the forbidden time", by paying a sum in lieu of the pillory, and the informer of this crime would get half the fine and half (the income from) the work. Wihtraed's law may be compared to Ine's (688—95), which prescribes that a "freeman" (i. e. a man conditionally free) who worked on a Sunday without his lord's permission should lose his freedom, "or he would have to pay a fine of 60 shillings and twice that sum to the priest.[11] This is an interesting sidelight on how a priest eked out his income. Ine also condemns slaves who work on Sundays without their lord's permission, and the punishment for this was

---

[10] LIEBERMANN I 13. Cf. also Æthilberht, LIEBERMANN I 25 ff.; LIEBERMANN I: Hlothheri and Eadric, 9 etc.; LIEBERMANN I: Wihtræd 12 etc.

[11] LIEBERMANN I 90.

scourging, but if he works at his lord's request he shall be made free and his lord shall be fined 30 shillings.[11] Alfred's laws largely follow the Mosaic law, for instance about Sunday: "Remember that thou hallowest the sabbath; ye shall work six days and ye shall rest on the seventh."[12] Although in many ways Alfred was a reformer, the bulk of the old laws had to be confirmed and he had to be cautious about innovations. Apparently he attempted to relieve the social position of the slave by letting him earn something (cf. Bosworth-Toller's Anglo-Saxon Dict.: *þeow*). However, the old system forms the basis of his laws. He allows all freemen to be free from work for 12 days at Christmas, and on the day when Christ defeated the devil, on St. Gregory's day, for 7 days at Easter, on the feast of St. Peter and St. Paul, and at harvest time for a whole week before St. Mary's feast, and on every holy day. Slaves and day-labourers (*esnewyrhtan*) were not allowed so much freedom. The slaves were allowed the Wednesdays in four fasting weeks, which they could choose for themselves, and on these days they were allowed to buy and sell and to earn money for themselves by working.[13] Plummer relates that Alfred had a great regard for impartial justice, so much so that he changed the precept in Exodus xxiii: "Neither shalt thou favour a poor man in his cause" — an injunction which was unnecessary in Alfred's time — into "Judge thou very equally; judge not one judgement for the rich, and another for the poor."[14] Even so, the basis of Old English society continued to be a system of slavery. The prohibition against working on Sundays is also kept in Eadweard's laws (921—38) and is even extended to bargainings and business.[15] The modern week-end may have its old, but forgotten roots in Eadgar's law (959—62) that the week-end may be free from work from noon-tide on Saturday unto the dawn of Monday.[16] Later not only work and business but also gatherings of people, hunting, and other affairs of the world were forbidden on Sundays by Æthelred (1008—11).[17] In another collection of the laws of Æthelred (992—1011) the slaves are

---

[12] LIEBERMANN I 26.

[13] LIEBERMANN I 78.

[14] See also PLUMMER, The Life and Times of Alfred the Great. Oxford 1902, 124 f.

[15] LIEBERMANN I 132. Cf. also LIEBERMANN I 164.

[16] LIEBERMANN I 198: noon-tide is here identical with the 9th hour of the religious houses, i. e. about 3 o'cl.

[17] LIEBERMANN I 252.

given freedom from work for three days before St. Michael's feast, that is, the Monday, Tuesday, and Wednesday before Michaelmas.[18] Canute (1027—34) also revived the regulation that no work or business should be done from "Sæternæsdæges none" to "Monandæges lih-tingce".[19] In another code issued by Canute it is stated that a man who worked on Sundays would be punished by being put in the pillory, or by a fine, but the serf would pay for it with his hide, i. e. a whipping.[20] Canute adds that the serf should be free, if his lord commanded him to work on a Sunday.[20] A Northumbrian law for priests (1028—1060) forbids not only work and business on Sundays, but also gatherings and all forms of transport either by carriage, by horse, or by carrying.[21] By this time the church had become powerful enough to enforce an almost Victorian sabbath observance. Eventually William the Conqueror con-firmed all the old laws as established by custom in different parts of· England: "Westsexelae, Merchenlae, Danelae" in the language of his scribes.[22]

The Old English peasant, although originally a free settler, seems to have suffered a social decline in the course of the centuries. The laws are not concerned with the independent peasant living on his own farm, but with peasants who lived together in villages. Large estates had apparently incorporated many farms which were originally free, and the peasants had become dependent on a lord. There was, of course, a constant process of change in society: some people sank, others rose. But the position of the peasant class in society was steadily sinking. The individual peasant was not wholly free. Dr. Whitelock quotes several instances from the 1040's where peasants could not leave their lord without his permission; even after his death the lord could dispose of them in his will.[23] Even so, they were looked upon as freemen. There

---

[18] LIEBERMANN I 260. — This habit still persists for labourers and maidservants in some parts of Sweden. Some scholars consider St. Michael's feast as a christianized heathen September festival.

[19] LIEBERMANN I 295. Here *none* means the original 9th hour of the natural day, i. e. about 3 o'cl.

[20] LIEBERMANN I 342.

[21] LIEBERMANN I 383.

[22] LIEBERMANN II 2: Mercienrecht.

[23] WHITELOCK, Anglo-Saxon Wills, p. 186, l. 14 (1042—3); p. 194, l. 4. "Wiking" (1045). Cf. also p. 112, l. 27 (c. 950). Cf. idem, The Beginnings of English Society. (Pelican Bks). 1952, p. 99 ff.

were many terms to describe a peasant: *ceorl, ceorlman, villanus, tunes-man, geneat(man), hiereman, inhiwan,* etc.[24] It sometimes seems as if the social differences in the lowest stratum of Old English society were as many and as subtle as those among the servants described by H. G. Wells in the early chapters of Tono Bungay. In general they lacked all rights of citizenship — they could not instigate legal action; there are even instances in which they were disposed of in a will along with the cattle and other property of their overlord.[25] The duties, work, and land-holding of the Old English peasant are described in a collection of Rectitudines[26] (960—1060). Of a lower rank than the peasants were the *cotsetlan* who had no farms, but owned only a piece of land and a simple cottage. According to Rectitudines the *cotsetla* had to work for his lord every Monday, or for three weeks every day during the harvest.[27] The freemen possessed some few things for their personal use; the freedmen (*freotmannon* or '*lisingar*') might keep their status of being freed when expressly said so by the owner and confirmed by witnesses.[28] In addition to these there were a number of half-free people.[29] The power and social rights of the lord are exemplified in a will of 1066, where the estate of Wereham is given with all the rights which the deceased had enjoyed, *and the men, both half-free and serfs and free men.*[30] A day-labourer (*esnewyrhta*) and a shepherd[31] were, perhaps, better placed than the serfs or slaves,[32] but the difference must have been small. To describe the social status of the lowest class it is enough to compare the slaves with domestic animals: they could be used as payment, inherited, sold, stolen, hunted, used to shield the owner, given back, exported overseas, their social position was in a word quite inhuman. The Church itself enjoyed and made full use of its rights over slaves which it had bought or inherited.[33] Often, how-

---

[24] LIEBERMANN II: 2, 297 ff.

[25] WHITELOCK XVIIm, p. 50 (964—980); ib. XVIII, p. 52 (1003—4).

[26] LIEBERMANN I 446; ib. II: 2 271.

[27] LIEBERMANN I 445.

[28] WHITELOCK X 13. (c. 950).

[29] LIEBERMANN II: 2: halbfreie.

[30] WHITELOCK XXXVI 11 (c. 1066); see footnote p. 206.

[31] LIEBERMANN II: 2: Hirten.

[32] LIEBERMANN II: 2: Unfrei; Verknechtung. Cf. WHITELOCK, The Beginnings of English Society p. 108.

[33] WHITELOCK XXXVI 11 (1066); LIEBERMANN II: 2: Kirchensklaven, Klostersklaven.

ever, the Church prepared the way for a better understanding of the
lot of these unhappy people.

The evidence afforded by Anglo-Saxon laws and wills is detailed
enough to show that the way of life of the so-called free men was little
removed from slavery. Still worse a bondman's, as seen in Aelfric's Col-
loquy (ed. Stevenson, Early Scholastic Colloquies. Anecdota Oxoniensis.
XV. 1929). "*Teacher*. What dost thou say, plough-man? How dost thou
go about thy work? *Ploughman*. Lo, my lord, hard work have I. I go
out at daybreak urging my oxen to the field, and I yoke them to my
plough. However stark the winter, I dare not lurk at home, for fear of
my lord. But when my oxen are yoked, arfd the share and the coulter
are fastened to the plough, each day I must plough a full acre, or more.
Teacher. Hast thou any comrade: *Ploughman*. I have a boy, urging
on the oxen with the goad, who, too, is now hoarse with cold and
shouting. *Teacher*. What else dost thou? *Ploughman*. Verily, I do still
more. I must fill the mangers of the oxen with hay, and water them,
and bear out their dung. *Teacher*. Oh! Oh! Great work it is. *Ploughman*. Yes, Sir, great work it is, for I am not free." The social conscience had yet to be awakened: the ruling classes had no sense of
social justice and the working class accepted more or less meekly the
unrelieved bitterness of life. Alfred's alleged division of the day was
not for such as these, — it was merely the personal discipline of a
scholar and a king.[34]

III.

William of Malmesbury, who lived from about 1090 to 1143, is
(according to Knowles p. 499) "unquestionably the greatest figure in
the English circle of lettered monks of the time ... He is the only
historical writer of his country and generation who can be read with
continuous pleasure and with unflagging interest, and this circumstance,
combined with the love of truth which he sincerely professes and dis-
plays, has put him in the forefront as an authority." J. W. H. Atkins
(English Literary Criticism. The Medieval Phase. London 1952, p. 92)

---

[34] It may be that Alfred did not invent the threefold division of the day, but in
the following pages I refer it to Alfred for the sake of convenience — without im-
plying that the rule was Alfred's own.

gives a striking instance of William's discernment in discussing "the mad fables of the Britons" concerning King Arthur, and praises his critical attitude generally; and both C. E. Wright (The Cultivation of Saga in Anglo-Saxon England. Edinburgh 1939; see pp. 30, 180 f., 233, 236), and R. M. Wilson (The Lost Literature of Medieval England, London 1952; see pp. 27, 52 f.) are of the opinion that William was a trustworthy collector of orally transmitted stories and songs, and, for his time, a conscientious chronicler. William was the librarian and chronicler of Glastonbury and Malmesbury, and during the years 1114—1123[35] he wrote a chronicle, Gesta Regum Anglorum, dealing with the Anglo-Saxon kings. At the same time the vernacular Anglo-Saxon Chronicle continued to be written up in several monasteries: Evesham, Christ Church, St. Augustine's of Canterbury and Peterborough. The Chronicle survived the longest at Peterborough, where the last entry is dated 1154. There were at the same time a large number of historical writers in monasteries up and down the country: Florence of Worcester (d. 1118), Symeon of Durham (fl. 1130), Geoffrey Gaimar (fl. 1140), Alfred of Beverley (d. 1143), Geoffrey of Monmouth (fl. 1154), and Henry of Huntingdon (d. 1155),[36] to mention only the most important. Their manuscripts were evidently copied and read in other monastic institutions, for it appears that William of Malmesbury (according to Knowles) knew Florence of Worcester and Symeon of Durham and modelled his style and matter on them. All these writers in their report of King Alfred's life, generally follow Bishop Asser's biography, although they do not always include everything, but pick out what seems most interesting to them. But in William of Malmesbury's account there occurs for the first time the information that Alfred made a threefold division of the day and night. He writes: "Finally, that I may briefly elucidate his whole life, he divided the twenty-four hours, that rotate together between day and night, in such

---

[35] See Willelmi Malmesbiriensis monachi Gesta Regum Anglorum. Vol. II. London 1840. ed. Th. D. Hardy, p. ix.

[36] Chronicon Florentii Wigorniensis, ed. Thorpe. London 1848. Tomus I p. 106, where only Alfred's six candles are referred to. Simeon of Durham, Historia Regum Anglorum et Dacorum. In "Opera": Chronicles and Memorials of Great Britain 75: a; only the candles referred to. Geoffro Gaimar, Lestorie des Engles. Chron. & Mem. 91. Alvredi Beverlacensis Annales sive Historia de Gestis Regum Britanniae Ed. Hearne 1716. Geoffrey of Monmouth, Historia Britonum. 1508 (1844). Henry of Huntingdon, Historia Anglorum. Chron. & Mem. 74. Only the candles referred to.

a way that he spent eight hours in writing, reading, and praying, eight hours in caring for his body and eight hours in dispatching the affairs of the realm."[37] As has already been observed, Asser never mentioned this in his biography; at least it does not occur in the version which has come down to us. It is difficult to see from what source William could have picked up this important detail, but it seems improbable that he should have invented the story himself for his fidelity to his sources is surprisingly consistent.

Such a division of the day could not have come down to William through a folk-tradition from "the Golden Age", for there is no evidence of its existence among primitive races.[37a] Nor, as we have seen, can the threefold division be derived from Antiquity, or from the monastic rules. Immediately following the passage about the three eight-hour periods occur the description of Alfred's invention of the six candles for measuring the time of day and night. But immediately *before* his account of Alfred's division of the day, William (following Asser) describes Alfred's system of dividing his revenue. His yearly revenue was divided first into two equal halves. The first half was divided again into three portions: one for his warriors and thanes, the other for the workmen in the employ of the King and his family, the third for strangers who visited them. The other half was further divided into four portions: one for poor people of every nation, one for the two monasteries he had founded (Æthelney and Shaftesbury), the third to boys of noble or humble birth attending the school he had established, and the fourth to monasteries all over

---

[37] William of Malmesbury, Gesta Regum Anglorum. Lib. II. p. 133. (Chron. & Mem. 90. London 1887): "Postremo, ut omnem vitam ejus breviter elucidem, viginti quatuor horas qua inter diem et noctem jugiter rotantur ita dividebat, ut octo horas in scribendo et legendo et orando, octo in cura corporis, octo in expediendo regni negotia, transigeret." Then follows the story about the candles.

[37a] E. ZINNER (a German astronomer), Tidsmaaling ved hjælp af Sol- og Stjerne-ure (Nordisk Astronomisk Tidsskrift. Copenhagen 1928, pp. 123—30), declares that sun-dials of Irish, and sometimes of Anglo-Saxon, origin in the first thousand years A. D., have their fields of figures divided into four parts, which indicates a division of the day and night into eight parts; this division, he says, was the usual one among the Germanic peoples and the Celts. — I am not competent to judge these matters, but the division into 4 (or 8) parts of the Ancient Germanic day (and night) is unknown to me and has not been proven by experts on Old Norse. In-stead there seems to have existed an approximate three-hour division in Christian Iceland: *eykt* (see NILSSON, loc. cit. 21).

Britain and Ireland. This may have confused William, but since he was an excellent latinist this assumption is not likely. It may well be that William was so influenced by the symmetry of the arrangement that he went even further and divided up Alfred's day into an equally attractive pattern. There is no denying that symmetrical arrangement had a profound influence on the medieval mind: the symmetry of material objects represented the ideal of perfection and finality. A threefold division had all the attractions of symmetrical arrangement together with the specifically Christian association of the Trinity. It was perhaps the most common of symmetrical divisions. Alfred, for instance, organised his realm into three orders of society: "A king must have men of prayer, men of war (fyrdmen), and workmen (weorc-men) ... Further he must have ... means of support for the three classes above spoken of" (Hodgkin, A History of the Anglo-Saxons. II. Oxford 1935, p. 595). In the Anglo-Saxon laws there are numerous instances of the magic of the figure 3.[38] When King Æthelred (992—1011) ordered his people to do penance on account of the invasion of the "Great (Danish) Army", the penance should last three days, people should eat nothing but bread, vegetables and water on Monday, Tuesday, and Wednesday before Michaelmas, from every farm they should bring to the church one penny (or goods to the value of one penny) and divide it into three parts.[39] In Cursor Mundi (c. 1300) this magical influence is still at work (10178): "In thrin his godes did he dele, / þat godd had lent him of his lane: / To pour part þan gaf he ane, / þe toþer part, als was for-melt, / It was bi-tuix þe prestes delt, / þe thrid parti was bikend / To þam-seluen for to spend". This may sound like King Alfred's division of his revenue, but it refers to "Sir" Ioachim of Nazareth in Galilee and his dame Anna; he divided his income into three parts: one for the poor, one for the priests, and one for them-selves.

Granted that such considerations sometimes led the medieval writers to construct something out of nothing, it would, however, be a grave mistake to assume that every detail owed its existence to a writer's

---

[38] LIEBERMANN II: 2 sub *drei*.

[39] LIEBERMANN I 262: Nu wille we þat eal folc to gemænelicre dædbote þrig dagas be hlafe 7 wirtum 7 wætere, þæt is on Monandæg 7 on Tiwesdæg 7 on Wodnesdæg ær Michæles mæssan ... 7 bringe man þæt to cirican 7 siððan on þreo dæle be scriftes 7 be tunesgerefan gewitnesse.

longing for perfection and symmetry. It is, for instance, to be wondered
at then that Asser gives instances of various symmetrical arrangements
— if they were such and had no reality behind them — and that the
threefold division is not emphasised by him. Further, it must be observed that William's so-called Alfredian tradition comes *before* the
description of Alfred's time measurer: it would have been more reasonable to have put it *after*. It would be farfetched to assume that William
was so influenced by such considerations as stated above that he actually invented the Alfredian legend about the three 8's. Medieval writers
often, it is true, paid little heed to what an earlier historian had
actually said and stated: they sometimes added small details to the
description of an historical event, sometimes even recasting the whole
situation, despite the fact that the only source for the later chroniclers
was the one they copied. Trevisa, among others, also protested against
the obvious exaggerations with regard to the Arthurian fable. But
to insert such a startling innovation into the life of Alfred without
any justification must be regarded as too much at variance with
William's usual pattern. Thus, for instance, William does not set out
to glorify King Alfred *à tout prix*. The well-known anecdote about
Alfred stealing as a minstrel into the Danish camp in order to spy, is
not told by William. On the contrary, he makes Olaf (Anlaf) Cuaran,
the Viking chieftain, perform that feat, *i. e.* stealing into the English
camp. (Wilson, loc. cit. 144 f.). The division into three eight-hour
periods was not inevitable, for only one of the divisions — that allotted
to sleep — represented continuous activity. The others were divided
up into a variety of occupations. In this respect St. Benedict's rule has
some affinities with Alfred's. It must, however, be remembered that
"the monastic threefold division is always of the *waking* life" (Knowles, p. 16 above).

   In Asser's biography it is stated that Alfred used to carry about with
him a small book in which he took down points of interest. This book
is completely lost. William of Malmesbury, however, mentions this
notebook: "which in the language of the country was called *Handboc*
(Encheiridion)", in Latin *Manualis Liber*.[40] It is tempting to suppose

---

[40] STEVENSON pp. lxiiv, 75, 153, 326; P. G. THOMAS, Cambridge History of Engl.
Lit. ch. VI, p. 91. WRIGHT (loc. cit. 21) and WILSON (loc. cit. 68, 74, 276: "We are
justified in regarding this (the Handbook) as a genuine lost work of the king ...")
do not doubt its existence. Wilson (p. 72) adds: "It seems to have been extant as

that in his *Handbook* Alfred had sketched a timetable involving a threefold division of the 24 hours. In planning his device of time-measuring Alfred may have realized that three such periods would be easy to measure and would form the basis of a satisfactory scheme of personal discipline. But, of course, there is no need to be too dogmatic about the impossibility of William inventing the division. Even so, does it matter if he did? It is still the Alfredian tradition even if Alfred himself never thought about it.

A later scribe of Malmesbury monastery, writing in French, has reconciled Asser's statement about the six candles burning down in twenty-four hours and William's statement about the threefold division of the day and night, for he writes: "This Alfred lived an extra-ordinary life. I will tell you briefly. The twenty-four hours between night and day he divided into three parts. Eight hours in writing, reading, and praying; eight hours in rest for the body; and eight hours in discourse and provision for the kingdom. He used to maintain a man in his chapel who served for this office, who divided the four and twenty hours by means of *three* (my italics. G. L.) equal candles. He burnt the first candle until eight hours had passed, and so on with the others. (Thus he called him) from hour to hour to do his proposed work. King Alfred also did more; he gave part of his lawful revenue to poor abbeys. He divided his revenues into two parts. One half he divided again into three parts; one part he gave to those who served in his court; the second part to those who wrought at his works; the third part to poor strangers. The other half he divided into four parts: one part he gave to the poor of his kingdom, the second part to poor religious houses, the third to poor clergy, the fourth part to poor churches in foreign parts." [41]

---

late as the 12th century when William of Malmesbury includes it amongst the works of Alfred".

[41] *Registrum Malmesburiense* (Chron. & Mem. 72), ed. BREWER. Vol. I. 1879. p. 54: "Cist alwred demena estrange vie, si uns durai breuement. Les vint e quatre oures ke sunt entre nuit e jour parti il en treis. Les vyt oures despendi en escriure, e lyre, e orer; les vyt en sun cors reposer, les vyt a parler del regne e purver. Si auoit un home en sa chapele ke serui de cel mester ke par treys bele chandeles departi les vint e quatre oures. Si fist arder la promere dekes les vyt oures furent passe, a issi fist des autres de oure en oure a fere sun purpos. Uncore fist plus cil Alwred. Il dona de sun dreyt purchaz a poures abbeyes. Si departi ses rentes en deus. La une meytie parti il en treis. La vne partie dona a ceus ke li seruirent en sa curt; la

This scribe, in jotting down a summary of Alfred's division of time and revenue, differed in several respects from what his celebrated predecessor had written, and in one respect he was quite ingenious: he found a link between Asser's accout of the candles and William's division of the day.

William of Malmesbury was the first to mention the Alfredian tradition that a busy man's day might well be divided into three equal parts for work, for the repose of the body, and for the good of his soul. It remains to be seen how this tradition was developed and maintained.

Stevenson (pp. xiv, lvi, lx) is of the opinion that Florence of Worcester copied the Asser original. William is said to have followed Florence's Asserian MS. Now there is no mention of the threefold division of the 24 hours in Florence, Symeon of Durham, Henry of

---

autre partie a ceus ke fesoyent ces oueraygnes; la terce a poueres estrangs. La autre meyte parti en quatre . . ."

Practically the same text is found in *Le Livere de Reis de Brittanie*. (Chron. & Mem. 42, ed. GLOVER, London 1865, p. 16): "Cist Alfred Amena estrange viʒe; si vus dirrai brevement. Les xxiiii. houres del jour e del nuyt despendist issi. Les viii. (hures en escrire e en lire e en orer, e les viii.) en son cors reposer; e les terce viii. houres a paireler e a poureance del regne. Si aveit un homme en sa chapele ki servi de cel mester, ki par treis owelles (equal, better than MS. *beles*, says the ed.) chandeles departi les xxiiii. houres. Si fist arder la primere chandele deskes viii. houres fussent passez; e issi les autres. Si sumunt luy de houre en houre de fere sun purpos." The editor believes *Le Livere* to be a translation from some Middle English Latin chronicler; it deals with English history to Edward I, or 1274. Its author might be Peter of Ickham (fl. 1290), a monk at Canterbury. Le Livere is apparently later than Registrum Malmesburiense.

Another French text appears in *An Anonymous Short English Metrical Chronicle* (EETS orig. s. 196), which evidently has the Malmesbury Register as its source. It runs as follows (ll. 305 ff.): "Apres lui regna le Rey Alfrede le plus sage rei qe unke pain manga il fist par la grace dieus tuz les bones leys dEngleterre. e puis vesqui e regna ici .xxviij. anz A Seint Paule de Loundres il est enterre. Celui rey Alfrede poi dormist en son lit pur ceo qil auoit grant trauaille. Les .xxiiij. houres qe sunt en la nuyt e en le iour ceus il departi en treis e il les empla mut bien. les .viij. il despendeit en prieres e en aumoines. les autres .viij. de reposer sun cors. les tierce .viij. furent les meillors. ceus il despendeit en penser pur sutiller coment il se purreit continer de endreiture sa tere guier. — Il i auoit vn home en sa chapele qe issi comenca les houres departire. Il fist treis chaundeilles par peis qe dussent arder par nuyt e iour. Quant la vn chaundele fu fet les .viij. houres furent fetes ensement. e par ceo il gar(da) le rei coment il dust son purpos a cher mener e issint vesqui le bone Alfrede. iesqes al houre quil morrust."

Huntingdon or Alfred of Beverley — who were William's contemporaries, more or less, — and they were followed by Roger of Hoveden "and the St. Alban's school of writers, whose influence upon medieval history-writing was all-pervading" (Stevenson p. 1). But on the other hand William of Malmesbury's chronicle was widely read in the Middle Ages. The dissemination of William's account was given a new impetus when it was incorporated into Higden's *Polychronicon*, a 14th c. work which, according to Bishop Stubbs, "stopped the writing of new books upon history and ensured the destruction of the old" (Stevenson p. 1 n.). In this way, William's statement became known to late writers and historians.

Among other medieval chroniclers who did *not* copy William's addition to Asser there are Ranulph de Glanville (d. 1190), Roger of Hoveden (d. 1201), *St. Neots Annals*, Johannes Historicus, Bartholomew de Cotton (d. 1298), John of Wallingford (d. 1258), John de Oxenedes (d. 1293), Walter de Coventry (fl. 1293), Robert of Gloucester (d. 1300), and Richard of Cirencester (d. 1401)[42]; nor is there any mention of it in the Brut (EETS orig. s. 131), which is merely a history of wars. William of Malmesbury's account is not mentioned by writers of the St. Alban's school. Roger of Wendover (d. 1236) who compiled Flores Historiarum beginning with the Creation and going up to 1135, was the chronicler of the monastery at St. Alban's; the mythical Matthew of Westminster, and Matthew Paris (d. 1259) continued the Flores. They do not refer to the threefold division, since their text follows Florence of Worcester closely.[43] John Capgrave, the Augustinian friar,

[42] Roger of Hoveden, Cronica (the years 722—1201). Chron. & Mem. 51: 1, ed. STUBBS 1868. St. Neot's Annals, ed. WÜLCKER, Anglia III. Johannes Historicus, ed. LUDEWIG's Reliquiae Manuscriptorum. Tome 12. Halle 1741. Bartholomew de Cotton, Chron. & Mem. 46, ed. LUARD. London 1859. John of Wallingford, Rerum Anglicarum Scriptores Veteres, ed. GALE 1691. — Wallingford's chronicle 449—1035. He was a monk of St. Alban's. John de Oxenedes, Chron. & Mem. 13. London 1859. His "chronicle of a chronicle" comprises the time Alfred the Great →1293, was written by a monk of St. Benet's Hulme, Norfolk. There the division of England into "hundraz" or "thethinges" was ascribed to Alfred. Walter de Coventry, Memoriale. Rolls series 58. I. 1872, p. 14: "Huic Alfredo non inveniebatur similis in probitate inter principes orbis, nec in sapientia." That is all about Alfred. His chronicle gives a very summary report of the times before 1066. Robert of Gloucester, Chron. & Mem. 86: I, ed. WRIGHT. London 1887. His chronicle ends in 1270. Richard of Cirencester, Speculum Historiale. Ed. John Ryland's Library. Manchester 1919; also in Chron. & Mem. 50, ed. J. E. B. MAYOR. Vol. II. London 1862 at p. 16 anecdotes about Alfred's early life, p. 39 about the candles. — Richard was a monk of St. Peter's, Westminster.

[43] ROGERI DE WENDOVER Chronica sive Flores Historiarum. Ed. COXE. Engl. Historical Soc. London 1841—44, & Appendix Flores Historiarum per Matthaeum

(d. 1464), is also silent on this point.[44] Other chronicles dealing with local subjects but throwing in now and then, a note of general interest about Alfred, such as the Annals of Waverley and of Dunstaple, also ignore William's account.

Turning now to the works which do repeat William's addition to the life of King Alfred, it is convenient to consult another MS from the monastery of Malmesbury: Eulogium Historiarum, which is supposed to have been written by a monk there and which begins with the Creation and continues up to 1366. Apparently several scribes combined to write this "eulogy". Although the writers very often refer to William of Malmesbury "(secundam Willielmum Malmsburiensem)", the first description of Alfred's life (vol. II p. 188) leaves out William's threefold division of the twenty-four hours.[45] But in chapter lxxxii (vol. III p. 9) there occurs the following. "This Aluredus (Alfred) divided day and night into xxiiii hours, according to Bede (sic), by burning candles in his chapel day and night. Thus eight hours (were devoted) to corporeal work with the affairs of the kingdom; eight to reading and writing and teaching, because the man was well-read in science; and eight to making prayers and (giving) alms." [46] An arrangement which left the king no time for sleep. Gervase of Canterbury (fl.

Westmonasteriensem collecti. Chron. & Mem. 84. Ed. LUARD. Vol. I p. 426 — corresponding to Stevenson's Asser § 100, p. 86. As will be seen from a comparison of the two texts, the St. Alban's chronicle sometimes expands and sometimes concentrates Asser's version. The Appendix (COXE's edn) I 322 corresponds to Stevenson's Asser § 76, p. 59, but shows rather important differences.

[44] JOHN CAPGRAVE, Chron. & Mem. I. A chronicle of Engl. history to A. D. 1417. p. 113: no reference to William of Malmesbury's statement. Cf. PLUMMER pp. 67—8.

[45] Eulogium Historiarum sive Temporis, ed. F. SCOTT HAYDON. Chron. & Mem. 9. I—III. II p. 188: "Viginti quatuor horas diei et noctis ita dividebat per combustionem candelae ut de singulis moneretur officiis sicut fecit Aluredus rex ut infra. Itam dimidiam portionem omnium censuum juste adquisitorum monasteriis suis delegavit, cunctos praeterea redditus in duas æquas partes dividebat; rursusque in primam in tres, quorum primam ministris suis curialibus, secundam operatoribus, quos jugiter in novarum aedium instructionibus mirabile modo habebat, tertiam advenis distribuebat . . ." This is said by the editor to have been written by another hand.

[46] Ib. III p. 9: "Iste Aluredus diem et noctem in xxiiii horis dividebat, secundam Bedam (!), per candelam ardentem in capella sua die et nocte. Octo enim horas in labore corporali circa regni negotia, octo in legendo et scribendo et docendo, quia vir literatus in scientia, octo in orationibus faciendis et in eleemosines." — The work was finished in Edward III's reign; deals with events unto 1366.

1188) seems to have had rather a colourless personality (Knowles p. 508), but he has apparently become interested in William's account of the division of the hours, for he quotes quite correctly: "He divided the twenty-four hours of the day and night so that he spent eight hours in writing, reading and praying, eight in rest for his body, eight in dispatching the affairs of his kingdom."[47] Another Gervase, Gervase of Tilbury (fl. 1211), also records William's statement.[47a] The Alfredian legend is also repeated by Ralph de Diceto (d. 1202).[47a] Although Piers of Langtoft (d. 1307) came from the north of England, he had evidently picked up the tradition of Alfred's division of the day. In his haltingly rhymed chronicle in French he notes that "Alfred lived in holiness all his time, / He spent the twenty-four hours of the night, / Eight in his prayers and eight while he slept, / The other eight in thinking, and in his heart provided / For the defence of his country that he might not lose it."[47b] Another French version of the Alfredian tradition is found in Peter of Ickham's (?; fl. 1290) chronicle Le Livere de Reis de Britanie as well as in An Anonymous Short English Metrical Chronicle.[41]

Ranulph Higden (d. 1364), the author of the Polychronicon, was a Benedictine monk at St. Werburgh's, Chester, where he would be

---

[47] Gervase of Canterbury, Chron. & Mem. 71. London 1879. II p. 45: "Viginti et quatuor horas diei et noctis ita diviserat ut viii. horas in scribendo, legendo et orando, viii. in cura corporis, viii. in expediendis regni negotiis transigeret. — Then follow the candles II p. 10 There are a few lines about Alfred as a legislator: ib. 36—39 Alfred is mentioned among other Anglo-Saxon kings.

[47a] Gervasii Tilberiensis De Impero Romano ... Commentatio, ed. MADERUS 1673. Radulfi de Diceto Opera historica, Chron. & Mem. 68 II, London 1876. p. 234: "Hic etiam xxiiii. horas quæ rotantur inter diem et noctem jugiter ita dividebat, ut octo transigeret in orando, legendo, scribendo; post in cura corporis octo; postmodum in expediendo regni negotia alias octo."

[47b] Pierre de Langtoft, Chronicle, ed. TH. WRIGHT. Chron. & Mem. 47. London 1857. I p. 315:

> Elfred tut sun tens saintement vesquit,
> Le xxviiij houre de la nout despendist,
> Viij. en ses priers, et viij. taunt cum dormist,
> Les altres viij. en penser, et de quer purvist
> De garder sa terre, ke il ne la perdist.

But Elfred is not Alfred of Wessex (but the rule is his); he is Alfred of Northumbria, who was buried at Driffield. On the other hand it seems as if the brother of the West-Saxon Alfred, Ethelred, had also been confused with the Northumbrian Alfred.

within easy reach of Malmesbury in Wiltshire, and also of Glastonbury in Somersetshire. It is quite natural therefore that William's addition to the life of Alfred should find its way into Ranulph Higden's work. William's version is given by Higden as follows: "And since he wanted to proportion his life rightly, he divided the twenty-four hours, which constitute the natural day, into three parts, of which he spent eight hours in reading, writing and praying, eight in rest for his body, and eight in state affairs. To be able to distinguish (the hours) he put in his chapel a candle of 24 parts so that as it burnt he should be warned by his church servants of his proposed work."[47c] There is a certain similarity between this version and those of Registrum Malmesburiense and Le Livere de Reis de Brittanie. The legend has evidently been corrupted in the course of the centuries: the French writers had reduced the number of candles to three; Ranulph Higden went one better: there is only one candle burning for 24 hours. But the three eight-hour periods are preserved. Higden's original Latin version had considerable influence among monastic historians. For instance we find in Liber Monasterii de Hyda[48] that the author quotes Higden profusely and copies almost word for word the passage referring to Alfred's division of the day. But the influence of Higden's Latin original was, however, relatively restricted compared with the wider currency of his work in translation. The Polychronicon was translated into English by John de Trevisa (d. 1412) in 1387,[49] and there exists another translation, too,

---

[47c] Ranulph Higden, Polychronicon, ed. LUMBY. London 1876. Vol. VI p. 362—63: "Et ut vitam suam æquilibraret, viginti quatuor horas, quibus dies naturalis integratur, in tres partes divisit, e quibus octo horas legendo, scribendo, orando, octo circa corporis curam, octo circa regni negotia transegit. Ad quæ distinguenda posuit in capella sua candelam viginti quatuor partium, quarum dispertita consumptione per ædituos suos de singulis prædictis moneretur." Cf. also ibid. p. 362: Secundam vero partem principalem proventuum suorum adhuc in quatuor pertes divisit, quarum prima pauperibus, secunda monasteriis fundandis, tertia scholaribus Oxoniæ congregatis et congregandis, quarta ecclesiis reparandis assignabatur. — Already in Higden the legend that Alfred had founded the university of Oxford turns up.

[48] Liber Monasterii de Hyda, Chron. & Mem. 45, ed. EDWARDS. London 1866. p. 45: "Et ut vitam (suam) rite aequilibraret, viginti quatuor horas quibus dies naturalis integratur in tres partes divisit: e quibus octo horas legendo, scribendo, orando; octo circa corporis curam; octo circa regni negotia, transegit. Ad quae distinguenda, posuit in capella sua candelam viginti quatuor partium, quarum dispertita consumptione per aedituos suos de singulis praedictis moneretur."

[49] Polychronicon, Trevisa: And for he wolde weie his owne lif ariȝte he delede

bearing the signum 2261.[49] The latter translation is not so old and dates from the 15th c. on the general evidence of spelling and language. These translations of Higden into the vernacular made the Polychronicon known to a wider secular audience and helped considerably in spreading the Alfredian tradition.

The tradition had sufficient intrinsic value to find its way into many works which were not directly concerned with Alfred. It was familiar for instance to Henry Bradshaw, who translated the *St. Werburgh legend* into English in 1513 (printed in 1521 by Pynson).[50] The translation was made expressly for common people, for Bradshaw says (Book I l. 80): "therefore I purpose / to do as I can: ... some small treatyse / to wryte breuely / To the comyn vulgares / theyr mynde to satisfy." At one point Bradshaw mentions the Alfredian tradition.

> This kyng (Alured) deuyded in .iiii. partes his richesse:
> One parte to the poore, the seconde to religion,
> the thyrde part to scholers, the fourth to bild churches;
> And of a day naturall he made trium diuision:
> viii. houres to rede and praye with ferucnt deuocion,
> viii. houres occupied with businesse naturall,
> and other .viii. houres to rule his realme riall.

*   *

*

The long working day of which Aelfric's ploughman complained, did not become shorter with the coming of the Normans, and under feudalism. But the influence of the Church preserved the "week-end"; for it might be imagined that when even the damned souls in Hell were

---

in þre þe foure and twenty houres of þe day and nyʒt, and spente eyʒte þerof in writynge and in redynge and biddynge of beedes, eyʒte aboute his body nedes, and eyʒte aboute nedes of þe kyngdom. And to departe þese houres rediliche he sette a candel in his chapel of foure and twenty parties, and schulde be i-warned of hem þat were i-ordeyned þerfore as ofte as eny of þilke foure and twenty were i-spend. — 2261: whiche wyllynge to spende his lyfe egally, dividede the dey naturalle into thre partes, disposynge viij. howres in redynge, writynge, and in preyenge, viij howres to the cures of his body, and viij howres to the utilite of the realme. To the distinction of whiche þinge he putte a candelle in his chapel of xxiiijti partes, and after the consumpcion of the partes he disposede hym to his ordinaunce.

[50] EETS orig. s. 88. London 1887. Book II, Part I, l. 358 et seq.

given a break in their pains "from non on saterdei, a þa cume monedeis lihting" (Zupitza-Schipper, Alt- und Mittelenglisches Übungsbuch, Wien und Leipzig 1912, p. 99, l. 78 f.; late 12th c.), ordinary live labourers may have enjoyed the same privilege. *Noon* may then have meant about 3 o'cl. — as it did in Anglo-Saxon times, — but may also stand for midday. NED quotes from 1303 (R. Brunne, Handlyng Synne): "þey shuld nat werche Lengyr þan þey rong none at þe chyrche", and classifies this as the 9th hour of the natural day. But, on the other hand, the NED quotations of 1290, etc., refer to midday. In the Calais ordinance of 1474 a division is made between ordinary Saturdays and Saturdays with vigils (work stopped at 15 o'cl.), on certain holyday eves at 19 o'cl. (summer) or 17 o'cl. (winter), and, lastly, on certain other holyday eves at 11 o'cl. (read 12 o'cl.); cf. below p. 42 ff. The ploughman had a long day, but modern research might say that it was not so remarkably long since much of the time was spent in tending, but no hard work all the time. It was partly just an easy going about; people had nothing else to do but care for the necessary things and jobs. It is possible, though, that at least young people sometimes wanted to have a leisure of their own, and felt tending just as fettering as hard work.

If we turn from agriculture to more industrial work, such as building, we meet, however, with the same conditions: the working day was just as long as daylight allowed it to be. L. F. Salzman has shown (Building in England down to 1540. Clarendon Press. Oxford 1952) that the building of churches, monasteries, castles, houses, bridges, etc., were not undertaken by the prelates, monks, lords, owners, corporations, etc., in such a way that they hired masons and operatives and carried on the work themselves. Instead, they arranged with master builders, who calculated the building costs, and, if agreed to, engaged the workmen and saw to it that the work was finished within a reasonable time — and certainly with profit (ibid. ch. 2). This implies that no slowing down on the part of the workers was allowed, — although conflicts arose now and then (ibid. pp. 28, 38, 55 ff.). But the organization was on the whole along modern industrial principles. It is interesting then to read the set of regulations for the craftsmen employed at York Minster in 1352 (ibid. p. 56 f.; orig in Latin).

"That the masons, carpenters and other workmen ought to begin work, on all working days in the summer, from Easter to Michaelmas, at sunrise and ought to work from that time until the ringing of the bell of the Blessed Virgin Mary, and then they should sit down to breakfast in the lodge of the works, if they have not breakfasted, for the space (of time that it takes to walk) half a league; and then the masters, or one of them, shall knock upon the door of the lodge, and all shall at once go to their work; and so they shall diligently carry out their duties until noon, and then they shall go to their dinner (*prandia*). Also in winter, from Michaelmas to Easter, they shall come to their work at dawn and everyone when he comes shall immediately start work, and so continue in the said way until noon. From the feast of the Invention of the Holy Cross (3 May) to the feast of St. Peter's Chains (1 August), they ought to sleep in the lodge after dinner; and when the vicars come out from the canons' hall (*mensa*) the master mason, or his deputy, shall cause them to rise from slumber and get to their work; and so they ought to work until the first bell for vespers, and then they shall sit and drink in the lodge, from the said first bell to the third bell, both in summer and winter. Also from the (1 August) to the (3 May), they shall return to their work immediately after their dinner, for which a reasonable time shall be taken, without waiting for the return of the vicars from the canons' hall; and so they shall work until the first bell for vespers and then they shall drink in the lodge until the third bell has rung, and shall return to their work, and so they shall work until the ringing of the bell of St. Mary's abbey which is called le Langebel, namely, every working day from the feast of St. Peter's Chains to Michaelmas, and from Michaelmas to the said feast of St. Peter, they shall continue to work as long as they can see by daylight. Also each mason shall take less for the week in winter, that is from Michaelmas to Easter, than in summer by one day's wage. Also when two feast days happen in one week, each loses one day's wage (*dietam*) and when three occur, half that week. Also on vigils and on Saturdays: when they rest after noon, out of respect for the next day, then they shall work until noon strikes ... And if anyone refuse to work in the said manner, let him be dismissed at once and not taken back again on to the works until he is willing to keep the rules in every detail."

The second set of regulations is from about 1370 in English (ibid. p. 57 f.).

"Itte es ordayned by ye Chapitre of ye kirk of Saint Peter of York

yat all ·ye masouns yt sall wyrke till ye werkes of ye same kyrk of
Saynte Petyr, sall fra Mighellmesse Day untill ye firste Sonday of
Lentyn, be ilka day atte morne atte yare werke, in ye loge, yat es
ordayned to the masounes at wyrk in with ye close bysyde ye forsayde
kirk, als erly als yai may sec skilfully by day lyghte for till wyrke;
and yai sall stande yar trewly wyrkande atte yar werke all ye day
aftyr, als lang als yai may se skilfully for till wyrke, yft(!) yt be
alle werkday; outher, elles, till itte be hegh none smytyn by ye clocke,
when haly day falles atte none, sauf yt in with yt forsayde tyme
bytwyx Mighelmes and Lentyne; and in all other tyme of ye yer yai
may dyne byfore none, yf yai wille, and alswa ette atte none whar
yaim likes, swa yt yai sall noghte dwell fra yair werkes in ye forsayde
loge natyme of ye yer in dyner tyme, bote swa schort tyme yat na
skilful man sall fynde defaute in yaire dwellynge; and in tyme of mete,
atte none, yai sall, natyme of ye yer, dwell fra the (ye?) loges, ne fra
yaire werke forsayde, ovyr ye space of ye tyme of an houre, and aftyr
none yai may drynk in ye loge: and for yaire drynkyng tyme bytwyn
Mighelmes and Lentyn yai sall noghte cese no lefe yare werk passand
ye tyme of half a mileway: ande fra ye first Sonday of Lentyn untill
Mighelmesse yai sall be in ye forsayde loge atte yaire werke atte ye
son risyng, and stande yare trewely ande bysily wyrkande upon ye
forsayde werke of ye kyrk all ye day, untill itte be namare space yan
tyme of a mileway byfore ye sone sette, if itte be werkday; outher elles
untill tyme of none, als itte es sayde byfore, saf yt yai sall, bytwix ye
first Sonday of Lentyne and Mighelmes, dyne and ette, als es byfore
sayde, ande slepe ande drynke aftyr none in ye forsayde loge; and yai
sall noghte cese no lefe yair werk in slepyng tyme passande ye tyme
of a mileway, no in drynkyng tyme after none passande ye tyme of a
mileway. And yai sall noghte slepe eftyre none na tyme botte bytwene
Seynte Elenmes and Lammes; and yf any mane dwell fra ye loge ande
fra ye werke forsayde, outher make defaute any tyme of ye yer agayn
yis forsayde ordinance he sall be chastyde with abatyng of his payment,
atte ye loking ande devys of ye maistyre masoun; and all yer tymes
and houres sall be reweled bi a bell ordayned yare fore. Ande, alswa,
it es ordayned yt na masoun sall be receavyde atte wyrke, to ye werk
of ye forsayde kyrke bot he be firste provede a weke or mare opon his
well wyrkyng; and aftyr yt he is foundyn souffissant of his werke,
be receavyde, of ye commune assente of ye mayster and ye kepers of

ye werk, and of ye mayster masoun, and swere upon ye boke yt he sall trewly and bysyli at his power, for oute any maner gylyry, fayntys, outher desayte, hald and kepe haly all ye poyntes of yis forsayde ordinance, in all thynges yt hym touches, or may touches(!), fra tyme yt he be receavyde till ye forsayde werke als lang als he sall dwell masoun hyryd atte wyrk till yt forsayde werke of ye kerk of Sanct Peytr, and noghte ga away fra yt forsayde werke bote ye maystyrs gyf hym lefe atte parte fra yt fersayde werk: and wha sum evyr cum agayne yis ordinance and brekes itte agayn ye will o ye forsayde Chapitre have he Goddys malyson and Saynt Petirs."

The dividing dates in 1352 were Michaelmas and Easter just as in the Statute of Labourers of 1349, while in 1370 they were Michaelmas and the first Sunday in Lent. But Mr. Salzman (ibid. pp. 58 f.) points out that the short day, with corresponding lower wages, was generally practised from All Saints (1 November) to the Purification (2 February); such is the case at various places in 1278, 1327, 1332, during the 14th c., and in 1530. But he does not say whether the working time of the 'summer' period was extended until those dates; possibly not. In many cases work had to stop in the 'winter' season wholly or partly for various reasons.

That the building workers were not allowed to slow down is seen in the ordinance drawn up for the masons and carpenters at Calais (then an English port) in 1474, according to which workmen had to pay fourpence for idling half an hour, and eightpence for idling one hour, to be deducted from their wages (ibid. p. 63). This document also gives rules for the working time. The workers should be at their work "every workyng daye from the fest of mychaelmas unto our lady daye in Lent as sone and tymely in the mornyng as the daye appereth and as they may see to werke and labor in the whiche he shall contynue unto xj of the clocke be stroken at none And to departe to his dynner, and by one of the clocke to be at his werke ageyne And so ther to abyde and labor as long as the day light will serve hym. And from our lady daye in Lent aboue saide unto the Fest of mychaelmas then next followyng dayly to be at his werke by halfe hour to v in the mornyng at the fardest And soo to contynue unto viij[th] of the clocke afforc none And then to have and (sic) hole houre and no more to brekefast and to come ageyne to worke at ix of the clocke and there to abyde unto xj of the clocke and then to departe to his dynner and to be ageyne at his worke by one of the clocke afftre none and there to worke unto iij of the clocke at after none and then to go to drincke yf he wyll and to be ageyne at his werke by iiij of the clocke foloyng and so to contynue unto vij of the clocke at even be stroken."

Then follow certain regulations concerning work at high tide and low tide, when workmen had to attend both night or day without any hours of rest or respite for the time to be taken. Then the following is added: "And for as moche as the saide carpenters and masons must allwey be redye and attendant upon every sodayne casualtie Rage and Chaunce that may happen to fall as well to the water workes by salte water or fresshe water or other wyse what some ever it be as well uppon the holy dais as uppon the workyngdais Therefore it is ordeyned that the sayde carpenters and masons shall be lycenced to leve work every Saturnsdaie in the yere that is no even to any Principall fest at iij of the clocke. And upon any even of pryncipall fest at none and upon any even that is Vygill at iij of the clocke at after none accordyng to the rule of the satursdais And uppon other sayntes dais hallowed nother even to pryncypall fest, Vygill ne satursdaye, to labor unto v of the clocke in Wynter from Mychaelmas to our lady daye in Lent and till vj of the clocke in somer season from our lady daye in lent at vij of the clocke and so unto mychaelmas folwyng." (ibid. p. 64).

The document proceeds to give important information about the principal feasts of the year, when work was to stop on the eves:

at 11 (= 12) o'cl. at noon: Christmas Day, Twelfth Day, Candlemas Day, Easter Day, Ascension Day, Whitsunday, Trinity Sunday, Corpus Christi Day, Assumption Day, The Nativity of Our Lady, All Hallows' Day, The Dedication Day of the Church (in Calais), St. Nicholas' Day.

at 3 o'cl.: St. Matthias' Day, Our Lady in Lent,[51] Midsummer Day, St. Peter's Day, St. Thomas of Canterbury, St. James' Day, St. Lawrence Day, St. Matthew's Day, St. Luke's Day, St. Simeon and Jude, St. Catherine's Day, St. Andrew's Day, The Conception of Our Lady, St. Thomas of India, St. Barthelemy's Day.

---

[51] This is confusing. Cf. above: "from our lady daye in lent at vij of the clocke ..."

at 6 *o'cl. in summer, at* 5 *in winter:* New Year's Day, St. George's
Day, St. Mark's Day, May Day, Holy Rod Day in May, St.
Mary Magdalene, Holy Rod Day in harvest, St. Edward's Day,
Michaelmas Day.

This is a most remarkable record. The working day in the 'summer'
period was consequently between 4.30 and 8, $= 3 \frac{1}{2}$ hours; 9 and 11
(read 12; see below), $= 3$ hours; 13 and 15, $= 2$ hours; 16 and 19,
$= 3$ hours; total 11 $\frac{1}{2}$ hours and 3 hours for meals. Besides, on the
eve of principal feasts (thirteen in number) work stopped at 12; on
the day of vigils, as well as on ordinary Saturdays, work stopped at
15 (fifteen vigils and ordinary Saturdays); on the eve of minor feasts
work stopped at 18 in summer and at 17 in winter (nine in number). This means another great reduction of the number of the
weekly working hours. Another startling item is given in footnote 5,
p. 78, in Salzman's work, where it is said that at Hampton Court in
1532 "9 hours were reckoned as a full day". The Calais ordinance
does not agree, however, with the set of rules practised in Edinburgh
in 1491 (ibid. p. 63, footn. 3), according to which working hours were
from 5 to 19, with breaks for breakfast at 8 ($\frac{1}{2}$ hour), dinner at 11
(read 12; 1 hour), drink at 16 ($\frac{1}{2}$ hour), totalling 13 active working
hours.

It is singular that at Calais and Edinburgh (cf. also NED *noon* 2
(1565): *11 houris at none*) 11 o'cl. is said to be the time for dinner.
Chaucer, Astrolabe (1391) writes most accurately: "from .xi *byforn*
(my italics) the howre of noon til on of the clok next folwyng."
About the middle of the 14th c. noon was identical with midday.
Mr. Salzman thinks of *high noon*,[51a] mentioned in the York ordinance
of 1370, and tries to explain 11 o'cl. in this way. But according to
NED *high* could be applied to midday, noon, undern, prime, etc., and
denoted completion: cf. NED *undern* 1 b. (c. 960): "From ærmorȝenne
oð heane undern (L. ad tertiam plenam)." Undern originally denoted
the 3rd hour of the day, but advanced to mean midday, then afternoon, even an afternoon meal. It is then puzzling to find as late as
1470 in Malory's Arthur: "Euery day ... from vnderne tyl hyhe
none ... three houres." When the Calais and Edinburgh authorities

---

[51a] Cf. 'höj midda(g)' in Vemmenhög parish, Sweden. S. LUNDWALL, Fataburen
(Stockholm) 1953, p. 164; and Old Icelandic 'hádegi' (12 o'cl. noon). Cf. O. Spanish
grant mannana and French *de grand matin*, where *grant*, etc., is not used like *high*.

	York 1352. 54°		York 1370. 54°	
	summer Easter-Michaelmas	winter	summer First Sunday in Lent-Michaelmas	winter
work begins	sunrise $^8/_4$ $^{20}/_6$ 5.17 3.27 $^{29}/_9$ 5.57 [1]	dawn $^{29}/_9$ $^{20}/_{12}$ 5.22 7.32 $^8/_4$ 4.50 [1]	sunrise $^3/_3$ $^{20}/_6$ 6.45 3.27 $^{29}/_9$ 5.57 [1]	»atte morne» $^{29}/_9$ $^{20}/_{12}$ 5.27 7.32 $^3/_3$ 6.12 [1]
breakfast	the bell of the Blessed Virgin Mary: $^1/_2$ hour	—	—	—
dinner	noon (midday) [2]	noon (midday) 'reasonable time' [2]	before, or at, noon (midday) as the workmen want: 1 hour [6]	before, or at, noon (midday), as the workmen want: 1 hour [6]
and sleep between $^3/_5$ and $^1/_8$	until the vicars come from dinner [3]	—	20 minutes	—
none-mete	between first and third bell for Vespers [4]	between first and third bell for Vespers [4]	20 minutes	10 minutes
work ends	le Langebel (at sunset?) $^8/_4$ $^{20}/_6$ 18.48+ 20.36+ $^{29}/_9$ 17.43+ [5]	as long as the workmen can see by daylight $^{29}/_9$ $^{20}/_{12}$ 18.18+ 16.22+ $^8/_4$ 19.22+ [5]	20 minutes before sunset: $^3/_3$ $^{20}/_6$ 17.40 20.36 $^{29}/_9$ 17.43 [5]	as long as the workmen can see by daylight $^{29}/_9$ $^{20}/_{12}$ 18.18+ 16.22+ $^3/_3$ 18.13+ [5]
Working hours	$^8/_4$ $^{20}/_6$ 13 $^1/_2$+ 17+ $^{29}/_9$ 11.45+		$^3/_3$ $^{20}/_6$ 11.45 17 $^{29}/_9$ 11.45	
meals (and sleep) a: $^3/_5$—$^1/_8$ b: $^1/_8$—$^3/_5$ Real working hours	2.20 1.50 11.40+ 14.40+ 10+		2 1.40 10 15 10	

Notes see p. 46.

Calais 1474. 51°.		Edinburgh 1491. 56°.	11 Hen VII 1495. 51—54	
summer Our Lady in Lent-Michaelmas	winter	summer	summer Mid-March—Mid-September	winter
4.30 o'cl. $25/3$ $20/6$ 5.33 3.39 $29/9$ 5.56 [8]	as the day appears $29/9$ $20/12$ 5.23 7.25 $25/3$ 5.18 [1]	5 o'cl. $15/3$ $20/6$ 6.17 3.12 $15/9$ 5.30	before 5 o'cl. $15/3$ $20/6$ 6.16 3.39 $15/9$ 5.33	the springing of the day $15/9$ $20/12$ 4.58 7.25 $10/3$ 5.39
8 o'cl 1 hour	—	8 o'cl. $1/2$ hour	$1/2$ hour	—
11 o'cl.struck at noon (midday) 1 hour.	11 o. cl. at noon (midday) 1 hour	11 o. cl. (mid-day) 1 hour	1 hour	1 hour
—	—	—	$15/5$—$15/8$ $1/2$ hour [10]	—
15 o'cl. 1 hour [9]	—	16 o'cl. $1/2$ hour	$1/2$ hour except for $15/5$—$15/8$ [10]	$1/2$ hour
19 o'cl.	as long as the daylight will serve the workmen $29/9$ $20/12$ 18.17+ 16.23+ $25/3$ 18.47+ [5]	19 o'cl	between 19 and 20 o'cl.	night of the day. $15/9$ $20/12$ 18.54+ 16.23+ $15/3$ 18.38+ [5]
14 $1/2$		14	14.45(?)	
} 3 11 $1/2$		} 2 12	} 2 12.45 (12.30)	

fixed 11 o'cl. for noon they acted certainly under the influence of the principles of the Benedictine rule, *i. e.* that the hours mentioned must be conceived to be complete: when the eleventh hour was full, it was noon.

In 1495 was enacted the statute which concerned working hours and which was to last more or less unchanged until the beginning of the 19th c., 11 Hen VII 1495 (c. 4). In comparison with the York

---

[1] Easter Day, 1352, was April 8. The First Sunday in Lent, 1370, was March 3. St. Elinmas (Helenmas), 1370, was May 3. Our Lady's Day, 1474, was stable: March 25. Michaelmas was stable: Sept. 29. Sunrise and dawn (civil twilight) are given for the first and the last day in the period, and for an intermediate day: June 20 and Dec. 20 respectively. It is evident from the 15th. c. ordinances and 11 Hen VII, when work began at a fixed hour, that sunrise, and dawn, must be regarded as an average time and not be interpreted literally. Cf. also BUTLER, speaking of the application of the Benedictine rule in Italy (p. 278): "the time was kept only in a rough and ready way; nor it is to be supposed that sunset and sunrise were accurately observed every day, and the length of the night and day hours calculated with astronomical exactitude".

[2] Noon in 1352 was at 12 o'clock. No length of dinner-time is given, but since all the other ordinances admit 1 hour, this may be inferred also in 1352.

[3] About half an hour must certainly be conceded to sleep. Cf. AELFRIC's young student, who says that in the monastery they sang midday (*sextam*), and then ate and drank and slept, and then they rose to sing noon (3 o'cl.). Cf. Colloquies p. 96.

[4] 20 minutes; cf. 1370. Vespers might have been celebrated at 16, or 16.15 o'cl.

[5] For dates and hours cf. 1). + after the figures indicates that work could go on for another quarter of an hour, or even half-hour. Cf. BUTLER p. 280 about work after sunset.

[6] The summer timetable of 1370 does not provide for breakfast. This may account for the stipulation that the workmen may have their dinner before noon. This circumstance (no breakfast) may also account for the early stop of the day's work: 20 minutes before sunset.

[7] Of remarkably short duration. Cf. 11 Hen VII.

[8] On March 23 sunrise is at 5.53. Thus 4.30 is very early. BUTLER says that when travelling in Southern Italy he noticed that workmen began work even before dawn. This early hour proves the existence of an average hour for beginning work; on June 20 the sun rises at 3.39. But 4.30 may also be due to harbour work, which had to be carried on all day and night. Cf. the acts (21 Ric II 1397—8, c. XVIII; 10 Hen VI 1432, c. 5) concerning repairs and strengthenings of the harbour.

[9] Very liberal.

[10] When the workmen were allowed to sleep in the period May 15—August 15, they were not allowed none-mete, and *vice versa*. — The whole 'sleeping' period has been moved forward a fortnight in comparison with earlier ordinances.

ordinances of 1352 and 1370 it sounds quite modern. The question whether labour conditions were aggravated through this law is best answered by comparing the ordinances of York (1352, 1370), Calais, Edinburgh and 11 Hen VII in a table. 11 Hen VII 1495 runs as follows.

"And ferthermore where divers artificers and laborers retayned to werke and serve waste moch part of the day and deserve not their wagis, sūmetyme in late coāyng unto their werke, erly departing ther-fro, longe sitting at ther brekfast at ther dyner and nonemete, and long tyme of sleping after none, to the losse and hurte of such persones as the seid artificers and laborers be reteyned with in service; It is therfor establisshed enacted and ordeyned by auctorite aforseid that every artificer and laborer be at his werke, betwen the myddes of the moneth of March and the myddes of the moneith of September, before V. of the Clocke in the mornyng, And that he have but half an houre for his brekefast, and an houre and half for his dyner at such tyme as he hath season for slepe to hym appoynted by this estatute, and at such tyme as is herin appoynted that he shall not slepe then he to have but an houre for his dyner and half an houre for his nonemete; and that he departe not from his werke, betwene the myddes of the seid monethes of March and September, till betwene vij and viij of the clocke in the evenyng; ... And that fro the myddes of September to the myddes of Marche every artificer and laborer be at ther werke in the springing of the day and departe not till nyght of the same day: And that the seid artificers and laborers slepe not by day but only from the myddes of the moneth of May unto the myddel of the moneth of August." (The Statutes of the Realm. London 1816.)

The working hours in the Early Middle Ages and in Anglo-Saxon times depended on the daylight. It is obvious that nightwork did not occur: only little work was done by candlelight. On the other hand, leisure was not allowed, or even thought of, except at the week-end, from Saturday noon (15 o'cl.) to early Monday morning and on certain Red Letter Saints' days. The daily routine lasted, then, from sunrise to sunset, or even a little later, in summer, and from dawn to dusk in winter. Now, since the planetary hours were twelve from sunrise to sunset, and from sunset to sunrise, quite apart from the astronomical length of the time units in various places and seasons, the balance of

4

work and physical recreation *seemed* to be fairly even. For the twelve
hours' work had further to be interrupted for meals, which reduced the
number of working hours to ten planetary hours. No doubt this
regulation continued even after the introduction of the balance clock,
but this invention brought with it an equal length of the hours whether
in the day or the night. Consequently the working hours seemed to
increase from the spring equinox to the autumn equinox, since the time
limits of the day were sunrise and sunset. But when investigating the
number of working hours of the Middle English period one must always
keep in mind that the notion of a day's work was, as it always had
been, from sunrise to sunset, — the hours were not counted. It is only
when we moderns look at it that we begin to reckon the hours of the
balance clock. At the end of the 15th c. a reform was carried through.
Instead of reckoning with sunrise and sunset, exact, or nearly exact,
hours of the clock were introduced, but on the whole corresponding to
sunrise and sunset. The number of hours were not given per day, or
per week; only the breaks for meals, and possibly sleep, are described
in half-hours and full hours. The summer half of the year is, of course,
easier to examine, for the winter half had no exact hours of the clock
to begin — or to end — work: the limits remained in the 15th c. as
'dawn' and 'nightfall'. It is no use, therefore, counting the free afternoon hours on Saturday and then deduct a number of hours from the
total of the working hours of a year, since working hours were not
added, or subtracted, in that way. People had to work as long as
daylight lasted: nobody questioned this wisdom.

But if we compare the figures of the real working hours during
summer the law enacted by Henry VII seems to lay down a harder
rule: the working day is between 12 and 12.45, meals deducted.[52] One
may, however, question whether this was an actual increase. Even in
our days habit turned into law seems to increase the burden of the
workers. For it must be remembered that the workmen themselves now
had a limit fixed for their exertions (although they could not appeal
if the law was infringed). It must be assumed that 11 Hen VII merely
confirmed a habit translated into clock-hours. Night work is not

---

[52] Encyclopædia of Social Sciences reckons the working-hours as from 5 a.m. to
8 p.m., which, allowing two hours for meals, makes 13 working hours. Steffen I 273
reckons 14 to 15 hours (minus meal hours). It is not expressly stated, however, that
the none-mete must account for half an hour also in summer time.

mentioned, although such a thing existed, — cf. Calais, and various other instances (cf. p. 62) in Mr. Salzman's book. But in general night work did not occur. The Encyclopædia of Social Sciences says that primitive lighting and the danger of fires determined the working hours. Many towns forbade nightwork. The gilds themselves were opposed to night work and summoned blacklegs before the courts for working at night.[53] The riots of the London apprentices in 1381 were aimed at the Flemish weavers because, among other things, they were said not to conform to the rules of the English gilds regarding night-work.[54] One source[55] says that the journeymen of the Middle Ages quarrelled with their masters about "Blue Mondays", i. e. a free Monday a week. This probably refers to some traditional weekly holiday. Apart from this there is no early instance of the term "Blue Monday" in the English dictionaries. A similar type of Monday is Cobbler's Monday (in Hazlitt, Faiths and Folklore II. 1905).[56] The lack of early quotations referring to Blue Monday is peculiar considering the frequency of *blaue Montage* in medieval Germany.[57] All workmen were, however, assured of one holiday each week by the insistence of the Church that no man should work after Saturday noon, and this holiday had been confirmed by the Old English laws and by the statutes of the Plantagenets. While the craftsmen of a gild were at least pro-tected against overtime, the labourers who formed the great mass of workmen in Medieval England, had only Saturday afternoon and Sunday for leisure.

The labourers had, then, to work 12 hours and more a day between the middle of March and the middle of September, except on Saturdays, according to the Act of 1495. In the winter half-year they had, in all probability, less, since field-work could no longer be carried on when the light failed. Thorold Rogers, Six Centuries of Work and Wages

[53] Cf. TAWNEY, Religion and the Rise of Capitalism. Pelican Bks 1938, p. 62.

[54] UNWIN, Gilds and Companies of London p. 138.

[55] Encyclopædia of Social Sciences.

[56] Black Monday (i. e. Easter Monday), although a religious holiday, is recorded in 1359 as a meeting day of a gild: Early Engl. Gilds (1870) p. 97: "This gild shall have by year four morrow-speeches (= a periodical assembly of a gild held on the morrow after the gild feast) ... the second shall be on Black Monday". See NED sub *mornspeech*.

[57] KARL KOEHNE, Studien zur Geschichte des blauen Montags. I. Zeitschr. f. Sozialwissenschaft 1920. Neue Folge. XI Jahrg. p. 268 ff.

(1908 edition, p. 180—81), maintains that for the artisan "the hours of labour were not long. They seem to have been not more than eight hours a day, and at a later period in the economical history of labour the eight hours' day seems to be indicated by the fact that extra hours are paid at such a rate as corresponds to the ordinary pay per hour for eight hours, being a little in excess." This refers to artisans. In the case of labourers he writes: "The medieval labourer took very few holidays. There is a general impression, that, previous to the Reformation, much of the labourer's time was wasted in the compulsory idleness of religious festivals ... it is certainly not true of mediaeval England." "The fifteenth century and the first quarter of the sixteenth were the golden age of the English labourer, if we are to interpret the wages which he earned by the cost of the necessaries of life ... Nor, as I have already observed, were the hours long. It is plain that the day was one of eight hours. Nor was the period of winter wages, when the pay was lessened, considerable, for the short-pay season is, when such a period is specified, only the months of December and January. Sometimes the labourer is paid for every day in the year, though it is certain that he did not work on Sundays and the principal holidays." (p. 327). It is difficult to reconcile this theory, which is based on pay-rolls, with the statutes and acts. Rogers's imposing work, which was first published in 1884, was probably influenced by his wish for a return to the alleged eight hours' day of the Middle Ages. Steffen on the other hand estimates the working day as ordained in 1495 at 14 to 15 hours: the labourer needed 8 hours' sleep and 1 or 2 hours for preparing work, and he suggests that the latter were perhaps counted as working hours. His considered opinion, however, is that life was tolerable enough under this system.[58] The red letter saints' days were used for work, says Steffen, for most probably the craftsmen worked on all days except Sundays *and* the red-letter day of their own patron-saint. Under this

---

[58] STEFFEN I 273. But Steffen is wrong when he says that 23 Hen VI regulates the day's work. This occurs only in 11 Hen VII (1495). Cf. also CUNNINGHAM 391: During the 15th c. the work of a summer's day lasted from 5 a.m. to 7.30 p.m. with breaks for meals, which may have been for 2 or 2 1/2 hours. He adds in a foot-note: "The long hours of which Aelfric's ploughman complained — who had to plough an acre or more in the day — would not greatly differ from those insisted on in the act of 1495." Aelfric's ploughman is apparently speaking of a day of the winter period.

system there may have been as many as 310 working days a year.[59] This is also confirmed by Walter of Henley (fl. 1250), who estimated the working weeks of the year at 44 for labourers in his Le Dite de Hosbanderye (ed. Lamond, pp. 9, 45): "You know that there are in the year fifty-two weeks. Now take away eight weeks for holydays and other hindrances, then are there forty-four working weeks left." That means a working year of 308 days. Walter, who had been a farm bailiff, also states that the labourer worked from the morning (i. e. sunrise) to 3 o'clock — in ploughing; other tasks awaited him later on in the day. Even allowing for a good deal of general slackness it is difficult to see how the long hours stipulated under the act can be reduced to the eight hours' day, which Rogers thought was usual in the fifteenth century.

Even the ordinances concerning work on Saturdays, and on the eves of the holydays, do not soften the picture. At Calais in 1474 work stopped at 12 o'cl. on 13 Saturdays, at 15 o'cl. on every ordinary Saturday and on the days of the vigils (15 in number), and at 17 o'cl. (in winter) and at 18 or 19 o'cl. (in summer) on minor holydays (9 in number).[60] Eves and vigil days make together 37. If we deduct this number from 365 we get 328; now deduct Walter of Henley's 308 working days from 328, and there are 20 ordinary Saturdays left. The actual hindrances (half-days except Saturdays) would than be 5. Mr. Salzman gives several instances of 'hindrances' to the employer, for instance (p. 65) that the workmen at Windsor in 1297 did not work on the Monday Oct. 7, St. Mark's day, because it was the day of the dedication of the local church. Cf. Calais. The building operatives in 1328 were paid for one day if there were two consecutive holydays

[59] STEFFEN I 271 (for the period 1350—1540): "Andererseits ist nicht anzunehmen, dass die vor der Reformation sehr grosse Zahl kirchlicher Feiertage für die Tagelöhner sämtlich ganz verloren gingen — denn, mit Ausnahme etwa der fünf grossen Kirchenfeste, stellte man die Arbeit wahrscheinlich nur auf dem Festtage desjenigen Heiligen ein, welcher Schutzpatron der *eigenen* Gilde, Kirche, oder Familie des betreffenden Arbeitsgebers war. So erklärt es sich, dass wir aus dem 13. und 14. Jahrhundert zuweilen bis etwa 310 Arbeitstage im Jahre für landwirtschaftliche Arbeiter und Handwerker erwähnt und dokumentarisch nachgewiesen finden."

[60] SALZMAN records an ordinance of Dundee (p. 64 footn. 1) in 1536 requiring work on every eve in Lent, but not on those of Xmas, Easter, Whitsun and the Assumption, till 16 o'cl. Ibid. (p. 65) is recorded that in 1539 workmen were supposed to work on Saturdays also between noon and evensong.

(p. 66). Sometimes, at York in 1371, they were paid extra for working
on a *pleghdai*,[61] the day on which they were sworn in (p. 78), and
they were also paid extra in the form of *closinghale*, ale drunk when
the roof of a house was closed (p. 79).

There is no doubt that the labourers and servants continued their
slow but dogged fight for better conditions during the centuries.[62] In
34 Edward III (1361) is found the interesting provision "that all
alliances and covines of masons and carpenters, and congregations,
chapters, ordinances and oaths between them made, or to be made,
shall be from henceforth void and wholly annulled". Mr. Salzman
quotes (p. 73 f.) an early instance of 1298—9 of organized resistance
against an ordinance on the part of the workmen; such was the case
also in 1331, when something like a strike occurred, and in 1339. 3 Hen
VI, 1425, c. 1 also forbids 'confederacies'. 'Assemblies', made on the
spur of the moment, to menace, or beat, their superiors were also forbidden to the workmen (1 Ric II, 1377, c. 6; 17 Ric II, 1393—4, c. 8;
11 Hen VII, 1495, c. 6). This shows that the workmen, whose wages
had also been regulated by the statute, had begun to organise their
resistance along the lines of trade unions. But in all the statutes as well
as in all the literature of the time, there is not the slightest mention of
working hours. There has been wrangling about wages, and payment,
but nowhere an instance can be found where the labourers or artisans
demand shorter hours. Organisation was the order of the day: witness
the gilds and crafts, but efficiency was certainly not aimed at. Cruel
treatment was given to men caught slacking by their masters, but it
may be assumed that a general slackness prevailed. The Act regulating
servant's wages: 11 Hen VII (1495), confirms that people who worked
only half a day should be paid for half a day only, and nothing for
holydays, which had been stipulated in 23 Hen VI (1445—6): "that no
artificer, workman, nor labourers, shall take anything (for the holyday
nor for the ferial day) but after the rate of the time of the day in which
he laboureth".

A week-work and a day-work are terms referred to already in the

---

[61] NED does not record so early an instance.

[62] An amusing example of this may be picked out of a Stonor letter (Stonor Papers,
Camden Soc. 3rd ser. 29. 30. 34. I p. 110) of the 15th century: we had "rather
break up households than have guests, for servants are not so diligent as they used
to be" — an early instance of an eternal complaint.

OE period — see Rectitudines in Thorpe's Laws ... I 234, A. D. 1000, where two days' work a whole year round, and in harvest time 4 days' work, is demanded from the *gebúr* (the land-tenant). Later a day's work was used in a transferred sense. Pecock (see NED) writes in 1449: "His day labor"; Shakespeare (Ric III 2: 1): "Now haue I done a good daies work." Coulton analyses the term in the light of old records and says: "... it is evident that a so-called 'day's work' had often been reduced to a half day of real honest labour. At Great Chesterford in 1270, each villain owed 714 weekworks, each of which occupied a quarter of his day. In addition, at ploughing time, he had to plough 16 ¼ acres. This totals at nearly three days a week."[63] And H. S. Bennett, who reconstructs life on a medieval English manor (1160—1450), is of the same opinion. He quotes a case: The Stoneley men in Warwickshire had to be in the field at sunrise and had to work until sunset. But this applied only to the harvest, says Bennett, for there are instances of such a long day being counted as 2 days' work.[64] These interpretations of how the law worked in practice may be true, but in later centuries where the evidence of working conditions is fuller and more detailed the general picture approximates to that outlined in the legislation of the 15th c. At any rate it is clear that neither employers nor employed had any notion of an eight hours' working day and the Alfredian tradition seems to have lain dormant. Nobody thought of it as a measure to be applied to practical politics.

IV.

At the end of the Middle Ages the art of printing had become known to Englishmen. In the 1470's William Caxton (? 1422—1491) had published several printed books, and several other printers were to

---

[63] COULTON, Medieval Panorama p. 73: "That principle was, that the serf possessed nothing of his own; yet he might enjoy his land so long as he rendered three days' work in the week to his lord in lieu of rent. Before those days of the later 13th century, when the multiplication of records enables us to get a far clearer view of the details, it is evident that a so-called "day's work" had often been reduced to a half-day of real honest labour." As to a day's work cf. NED: DARG, DARGER, DARKER, DARGSMAN, DARGING, DAYING, DAY-LABOUR, DAY-LABOURER, DAY-LABOURING, DAY-MENT, DAYSMAN 2, DAYTAL, DATEL, DATELLER.

[64] H. S. BENNETT, Life on the English Manor ... 1160—1450, p. 104.

follow him. Caxton availed himself of extant medieval manuscripts, which were made public to an ever increasing circle of readers. His choice of MSS was that of a commercial printer and publisher and included philosophy, versified stories, a chess manual, grammars, and chronicles, — all of which were books that would sell. These early printers also played an important part in furnishing the reading public with stories and chronicles which formed a link between the literature of olden days and the coming generation of poets and dramatists, who were thus able to enjoy, or criticise, or steal, from the works of their predecessors. The 14th c. had been a most flourishing period of English literature, and the printers saved it from oblivion. In the works of the Elizabethans the names of medieval writers (Chaucer, Gower, Higden, etc.) occur, showing that the writers of the Tudor-Stuart period were familiar with the 14th c. authors.

There was another literary movement, however, no doubt inspired by the Humanism of the epoch. While some — and the majority — dug deeply in Classical literature and civilization and thus enriched the English way of thinking and writing, there were several who turned to native sources, the medieval chronicles in Latin, or English, and published them. Their method of editing was not exact and scholarly, — still too much of the medieval disregard for accuracy and the medieval fancifulness lingered. However, they served a useful purpose in making educated people acquainted with the early history of England and in this way exciting their patriotic spirit.

The interest in Alfred the Great after 1600, which can be, almost statistically, studied in the dramas, epics, poems, and later in prose stories, is indubitably to be ascribed to the activities of the editors of the old chronicle texts.[65] As a by-product they also furnished later

---

[65] See LOUIS WARDLAW MILES, King Alfred in Literature. Baltimore. 1902. p. 114 f. — I have gone through most of the works mentioned there. Alvredus, sive Alfredus. Tragico-Comoedia (in 5 acts, and in verse) by Gulielmus Druraeus (William Drury), Douai 1620. It is an intolerably boring play with long speeches in Latin; Alfred's whole family appears, beside St. Cuthbert and St. Neot. Robert Powell of Wels, The Life of Alfred or Alured. London 1634, has not been accessible to me. R. Kirkham, Alfred or Right Reenthroned, 1659, deals with the Danish king Gothurnus and his victory over Alfred, who disguises himself as a minstrel and steals into the Danish camp, and finally wins a decisive victory over the Danes. Sir Richard Blackmore's Alfred. An epick Poem. 1723: The twelve books are a eulogy of the monarch. Thomson and Mallets Alfred: A Masque (1740), and Alfred the Great, A Drama for Music, new composed by Mr. Arne (1753) exalt Alfred's character;

writers with "the matter of Denmark and Norway" (not only with "the matter of England"), because the material in the old chronicles also dealt with the wars between the English and the Vikings, and so we can regard them as being forerunners of the later editors of Icelandic texts. The popular chroniclers, later elevated to the rank of historians, benefited from the matter retold by the editors of medieval historical texts and incorporated it into their own books.

Caxton printed the Polychronicon twice, the first edition in Trevisa's translation in 1480 and the second in 1482; another printer, Wynkyn de Worde, also published Trevisa's version in 1495; and later still, Peter Treveris published the same version in 1527. In all these Alfred's threefold division of the 24 hours was made known to the public. In 1548 Bishop Bale (1495—1563) published (in Basle, Switzerland) Illustriu(m) maioris Brytanniae Scriptorum ... Summarium; a second edition (extended) followed in 1557—59. In his edition of Asser's biography, which serves for the life of Alfred in this collection, we find in the 1st edition (p. 115): "For eight hours he himself spent daily in reading, writing, dictating and praying, and he urged all and sundry to virtue and literary studies, both commons and nobles, both women and men."[66] It is evident that Bale allowed himself some alterations of the source.

Alfred the Great, Deliverer of his Country, by the author of The Friendly Rival; A. von Haller, Alfred, König der Angel-Sachsen (1773); John Home, Alfred. A Tragedy (1777); author's preface: "The Hero, critics have said, is degraded to a Lover and is not a legislator. But the author permits himself to bend his arches, and finish the fabrick, according to his taste and fancy, for the poet is at liberty and it is the essence of his art, to invent such intermediate circumstances, and incidents, as he thinks will produce the most affecting situations"; J. Ryland, The Life and Character of Alfred the Great (1784); Ebenezer Rhodes, Alfred. An historical Tragedy (1789); Anonymous, Alfred: An Historical Tragedy (1789); Lonsdale, Sketch of Alfred the Great: or the Danish Invasion (1798); Joseph Cottle, Alfred and the Fall of Cambria (1801); (Rev. J. Sympson?), Science Revived, or the Vision of Alfred. A Poem in Eight Books (1802); John Penn, The Battle of Edington or British Liberty. A Tragedy (1832); A. M. S. (Agnes M. Stewart), Stories about Alfred the Great (1840); John A. Giles, The Life and Times of Alfred the Great (1848); Thomas Hughes, Alfred the Great (1869); all these books deal with Alfred's wars against the Danish vikings and do not contain any reference to Alfred's threefold division of the twenty-four hours.

[66] "Nam octo horas & ipse quotidie, legendo, scribendo, dictando, et orando transigebat, omnesq ad uirtutum se literarum studia, tam uulgares quam nobiles, tam foeminas quam uiros prouocabat."

Archbishop Matthew Parker (1504—75) was a keen antiquarian and showed
his interest by printing Gilda, Asser, Aelfric, Flores Historiarum, Matthew Paris,
and other chronicles and texts. In 1574 there appeared Asser (Joannes) Menevensis,
Bishop of Sherburn Aelfredi regis res gestae, which also contained the will of King
Aelfred and the preface to his translation of St. Gregory's Pastoral Care. The 'Res
Gestae' and the will were in Latin, but printed in Anglo-Saxon characters, while the
preface to the Pastoral Care was in Anglo-Saxon with an interlinear translation in
English, followed by a Latin translation. Archbishop Parker printed Asser from the
then only extant Asser MS., which has since perished. In his edition of Asser, Parker
showed lack of scholarship by interpolating details from the Annals of St. Neot, but
he acted in good faith.[67] Henry Sweet says that "the study of Old English was first
revived by Archbishop Parker", but although W. H. Stevenson does not deny this,
the latter is, naturally, critical of Parker's edition of the text.[68] The passage about
the invention of the candles as time-measurers, however, is taken over by Stevenson
from Parker's text intact as being probably authentic Asser. There is consequently
no reference to Alfred's threefold division of the twenty-four hours. Nor is there in
John Stow's edition of Matthew of Westminster's Flores Historiarum and Matthew
Paris (1571), neither in Jerome Commelin: Rerum Britannicarum, id est, Angliae,
Scotiae ... (Heidelberg 1587), where the emphasis lies more on French and Norman
affairs than on English. A new edition of Florence of Worcester in 1592 did not
bring any detail on Alfred's division of the day.

With Sir Henry Savile (1549—1622) the legend, however, appears
again. In 1596 (London) and 1601 (Frankfort) he published several
old chronicles under the title Scriptores post Bedam. Among others we
find Florence of Worcester, Matthew of Westminster, Ethelwardus,
Henry of Huntingdon, Roger of Hoveden, (all of whom had not mentioned Alfred's three 8's), but also the account of William of Malmesbury, who had been the first chronicler to state that Alfred had
instituted the rule of the "eight hours' day", was printed in full.[69]
Another document of disputed origin, but printed by Savile, is De-
scriptio compilata par dominum Ingvlphum abbatem monasterii Croy-
land ... To-day there is no doubt about its being a later forgery, but
from our point of view this is not relevant. Forgery or no forgery, the
chronicle's words about Alfred's working-day were at that time believed, copied and spread by many people (p. 870 in Savile's ed.):

---

[67] See CHAMBERS, England before the Norman Conquest, p. 201.

[68] HENRY SWEET, Gregory's Pastoral Care. Transl. by King Alfred. 1871. p. vi. —
STEVENSON, Asser's Life of King Alfred. Oxford 1904. p. xv—xxi & passim.

[69] SIR HENRY SAVILE, Rerum Anglicarum Scriptores Post Bedam ... nvnc primvm
in lucem editi. Francofurti MDCI: Willielmi monachi Malmesbvriensis de gestis
regum anglorum lib. II, cap. 4, p. 45 (for the quotation, see p. 28, footn. 37).

"Prescribing for himself, too, a regular life he spent daily, from early morning, eight hours in divine service. For in his chapel he had a waxen candle constantly burning in front of the relics of the saints, divided according to those three eights, and a servant was appointed to remind the king in a loud voice, instead of a clock, of the portion due next when each of the portions had been consumed."[70]

In 1602 William Camden, the well-known antiquarian, published De Aelfredi Rebus Gestis, in which he followed Asser. The text seems to be exactly the same as Parker's, except that instead of using Anglo-Saxon characters it uses Roman ones. Camden's work Anglica, Normannica, Hibernica, Cambrica a veteribus scripta (1603) does not contain any reference to Alfred's hours. Neither does Johannis Rossi (I) De Regibus Veteris Britanniae usque ad exitium gentis & Saxonum imperium, dedicated to James I (1607). The book is a tedious account dealing mainly with legendary figures of the Celts and Romans, and in some cases with historical people, but it does not mention Alfred. [Bede's History of the Old English Church was printed at Cologne in 1612 (Knowles p. 494).]

In 1673 Maderus, a German scholar, incorporated in Otia Imperialia Gervasii Tilberiensis De Impero Romano Commentatio, which records Alfred's division of the day. Sir John Spelman (1564—1641), who represents a new type of scholar, weighing the historical material with critical judgment, published a glossary of Obsolete Latin and Old English terms (2 vols.) in 1626, and his other great work, Aelfredi Magni Anglorum Regis Invictissima Vita, was published in 1678, after his death, by his friends. The work is magnificent. In Book III, p. 162, § 79, we read: "Further it should be noted that there is a certain discrepancy between Asser Menevensis and (William of) Malmesbury as to the quantity of the time that Alfred promised to devote. The former records what we have quoted above,[71] but the latter that he divided the twenty-four hours into three portions, and he is said to have devoted the first of these to God, the second to the affairs of the

---

[70] Sibimet ipsi etiam vitam regularem indicens quotidie a summo (summu) mane per octo horas diuino seruitio vacabat. Habebat enim in capella sua cereum coram sanctorum reliquiis continue ardentem secundum haec tria octonaria proportionatum; ministrumq institutum, qui singulis portionibus consumpti(s) & consummatis, regem de succendente portione dice horologij voce viua commonebat. Cf. REINHOLD PAULI, König Aelfred. Berlin 1851, p. 16; LAPPENBERG, Geschichte von England. Hamburg 1834, p. lxii, where he doubts the authenticity of Ingulph in view of his ignorance of contemporary events, but ends by accepting him; Miles p. 34.

[71] See p. 19 f.

realm, and the remaining to natural refreshment and sleep, and that, consequently, he is said to have devoted only a third of his time to God. Which opinion merits rather to be trusted, the reader may himself determine: both are, indeed, represented by good authors. Asser, however, not only assisted the King, but he was also privy to his promise, and the lack of accordance between them is not so great, since, also according to Asser, it is evident that the promise was made with certain limitations, that is to say, to be kept only with regard to his weak health, chances, and circumstances. This might, indeed, limit (the time) to the quantity (William of) Malmesbury states." In footnote 1 on the same page Spelman adds: "(Wm of) Malmesbury seems to have taken his account from Ingulf: I shall with pleasure reproduce the whole passage (although several things are lacking in the printed edition) from the excellent codex MS⁰, which the widely renowned Johannes Marsham, both in nature and studies a son of Master John, showed me when taking this down: He prescribed for himself an accurately divided life, and hence he devoted daily, from early morning, eight hours to the divine service. Then he was busy with the affairs of the realm for eight hours, and finally he paid due attention to the wants of his body during the last eight hours of the natural day. For in his chapel, in front of the relics of the saints, he had a permanently burning wax-candle notched according to three eighths, and a servant, who, when each part had burnt down and was finished, in a loud voice reminded the King of the next part." [Porro notandum est, Asserium Menevensem à Malmesburiensi nonnihil discrepare circa temporis modum, quod Ælfredus devovit. Priore quod supra posuimus tradente: posteriore vero, quod 24 horas in tres portiones partitus earum primam Deo consecrarit; secundam rebus Regni publicis; reliquam naturali refectioni, & quieti; adeoque tertiam tantum temporis partem Deo dedicarit. Utri sententiæ potior fides adhibenda sit, penes lectorem restabit judicium: utraque certe idoneos autores habet.[72] Asserius autem non tantum Regi

---

[72] Malmesburiensis ex Ingulfo narrationem suam hausisse videtur: locum integrum (cum in impresso aliqua desint) ex optimæ notæ codice Ms⁰, quem nobis hæc scribentibus præstitit clarissimus Johannes Marsham Domini Johannis tum natura tum studiis F. reddere non pigebit. *Sibimet ipsi vitam regularem indicens quotidie à summa mane per octo horas divino servitio vacabat. Deinde per octo horas alias Regni negotiis intendebat, demum per octo horas diei naturalis novissimas curam sui corporis procurabat. Habebat enim in capella sua cereum coram sanctorum reliquiis*

superfuit, sed & eidem voti conscius; neque valde pugnant hæc inter se: cum ex ipso Asserio constet votum non sine certis exceptionibus factum, quantum scilicet infirmitas, possibilitas, & suppetentia permitterent. Quæ praxi facile intra modum, quem refert Malmesburiensis, coarctarentur].

Spelman did not know that Ingulph's was a spurious document. The source of the forger of Ingulph's chronicle must have been the description in Registrum Malmesburiense or Le Livere de Reis de Britannie (see p. 31 footn. 41) or some other document not accessible to us; it is also possible that he garnished the story told by Higden and Trevisa, who added that Alfred employed a certain servant to watch the burning of the candles. Anyhow, the legend was once again repeated by Spelman, and survived in a later edition of his work. W. Fulman also printed Ingulph's chronicle in his work Rerum Anglicarum Scriptorum Veterum (vol. I; there was no II), printed in Oxford in 1684.

Another editor of old documents was Thomas Gale (? 1635—1702). He published in 1687 Historiae Anglicanae Scriptores, and in 1691

---

continue ardentem secundum hæc tria octonaria proportinatum; ministrumque institutum, qui singulis portionibus consumptis & consummatis Regem de succedente portione vita horologii voce viva commonebat.

Spelman's work was translated and edited by Thomas Hearne: John Spelman, The Life of Aelfred the Great. With considerable additions (!) ... By the Publisher Thomas Hearne. Oxford 1709. p. 206 (§ 90): "It is to be noted that there is a difference between the Relation of Asser Men. and Malmesbury concerning the quantity of the time that Aelfred devoted, the first alledging as we have already delivered, the other that he divided the 24 hours into three parts, and that the first of them he devoted to God, the second to the affairs of the kingdom, and the third to his natural Refreshment and Rest, and so gave but a third part of his time to God. Which of the two shall be believed rather will be in the reader's opinion to determine: both are very creditable authors, but Asser not only lived in Aelfred's time, but was privy to the making of the vow. And it is not impossible that both were true. For it appears by Asser that the vow was with some limitation, and saving to the duty of his calling, to the necessity of his occasions, and to the strength of Nature, which in practice might well be brought unto the proportion that Malmsbury delivers. § 91. It is further considerable concerning this vow of the King's that it was made, neither in the time of his adversity, (when everybody is religious), nor yet in his old age, when the world had first forsaken him; but as he began his religious practices even in the prime of his youth, so this vow was the free oblation of his heart in the strength of his years; and in the height of his success, and fruition of God of all his passed labours, soon after he had built the monastery of Aethelingaey in performance of his vow for his victory at Aethandune.

Historiæ Britannicæ, Saxonicæ, Anglo-Danicæ, Anglicanæ Scriptores
XV (Oxon 1691). Stevenson (p. 115) is not satisfied with his editing
of Asser's biography, which Gale called Chron. Fani Sancti Neoti
sive Annales Joan. Asserii. What is of interest in this book is that Gale
also included Higden's Polychronicon, and thus (ibid. p. 257) printed
the passage about the three equal portions of the natural day ascribed
to Alfred. Thomas Hearne (1678—1735) — a scholar with ardent
antiquarian interests to whom Pope refers in Moral Essays, Ep. IV l.
9: "Rare monkish Manuscripts for Hearne alone", — issued several
editions of ancient manuscripts and 16th and 17th c. writers on English
history, such as Camden (1717) and Spelman (1709); he also brought
to light Joannis Rossi (II), (the name spelt Rous or Rovs), Antiquarii
Warwicensis Historia Regum Angliae. Both in the translation of Spelman's work (see p. 59 footn. 72) and in the version of Rous's chronicle[73]
we meet again the statement that Alfred divided his day and night
into three equal parts of eight hours each. In 1732 Otterbourne's medieval
chronicle De Rerum Anglicarum, extending to 1420, was printed by
Hearne, in which the Alfredian tradition is repeated (p. 49): "He also
spent eight hours every day in writing, reading, and praying, eight
hours he spent in the care of his body, and the other eight hours were
used for the affairs of his kingdom". Again on p. 52 reference is made
to this threefold division in exactly the same words.[74]

    Another editor of old texts was Joseph Sparke, Historiae Anglicanae
scriptores varii, e codicibus manuscriptis nunc primum editi. London
1723. The first work included in this collection is Chronicon Johannis
Abbatis S. Petri de Burgo (Anno DCCCLXXII), of which the following

---

[73] Rossi, 2nd ed., Oxford 1745 (p. 76): "Rex Aluredus alias Alfredus, miles proba-
tissimus, sapientia alter Salamon ... Istius regis diebus, ut videtur, non erant, ut
modo, in ecclesiis nobilium urbium civitatum & villarum horologia, ut modo habentur;
sed ipse pro parte sua ordinavit de cera tres pro qualibet die, quarum quaelibet
accensa octo horis ardere veraciter vellet unum octanarium (octonarium) expande-
bant in dei servicis, secundum in causis temporalibus audiendis, & corporis cibo &
potu, recreatione, & tercium nocturna expandebat quiete per candelas accensas certa
determinatione."

[74] (p. 49): "Hic etiam octo horas omni die in scribendo, legendo et orando transegit, octo horas in cura corporis consumpsit, & alias octo horas circa regia negotia
expendebat. — p. 52: Hic enim Elfredus ... 8 horas omni die in scribendo, legendo,
orando, transegit, 8 horas in cura corporis consumpsit, et alias 8 horas circa regia
negotia expendebat.

extract is relevant (p. 22): "Ipse (i. e. Alfredus) ...: omnis (sic cod.) etiam diei naturalis dividebat in tria octonaria juxta mensuram & metam cujusdam cerei jugiter in capella sua coram sanctorum reliquiis ardentis, & dicta tria octonaria designantis; in quorum primo, videlicet a summo mane usque ad plenam ... sextam diei divino servitio vacabat; in secundo octonario consiliis ac negotiis regni sui intendebat; in tertio vero corporis sui necessitatibus indulgebat." Here we have the words that the period of divine service ended at noon; another period of work continued for eight hours, i. e. until 8 o'clock p.m., and then sleep and other recreation for another eight hours, i. e. 4 a.m., so that Alfred's divine service began at 4 a.m The system is thus worked out in detail.

On the other hand, J. P. Ludewig's collection of printed MSS, Reliquiae Manuscriptorum (Tome 12. Halle/Saale 1741) also contains Johannes Historicus, Angliae Chronicon, which deals with Alfred but does not mention the threefold division. Finally, Francis Wise (1695—1767) printed an edition of Archbishop Parker's Asser: Asser, Annales Rerum gestarum Aelfredi Magni. Oxford 1722, in which Wise took care to mark out what he considered to be interpolated from St. Neot's annals. Wise's edition was prepared again for publication by H. Petrie (1768—1842) and J. Sharpe, and printed by Th. D. Hardy in 1848: Asserius de Rebus Gestis Aelfredi (Monum. Hist. Brit. I, p. 496 ff.), which is identical with Parker's edition and consequently does not give the passage about Alfred's division of the day.

Among the chroniclers and historians there are some who reproduce William of Malmesbury's statement, and some who do not.[75] Robert

---

[75] No references to Alfred's threefold division of the natural day in Polydore Vergil's Anglicæ Historiæ Libri XXVI, Basle 1534: John Hardyng's rhymed chronicle (ed. H. Ellis 1812); Cooper, An Epitome of Chronicles (Cooper's Chronicle) 1565 (a bald narrative of events); Harvey, Philadelphus, or a Defence of Brutus and the Brutans History. 1593; Grafton's several chronicles 1562, 1568, 1611 (1809), including Hardyng's Chron. 1543, and Hall's Union 1548; John Leland's Itinerary, ed. Smith in 5 vols. 1906—10; Richard Verstegan (= Richard Rowlands), Antiquities concerning the English Nation, 1605; Sir Walter Ralegh's General History of the World; Michael Drayton's Poly-Olbion. 1622; Roger Twysden, Historiae Anglicanae scriptores X. 1652; Daniel Langhorn, Chronicon Regum Anglorum (1689), — only to 819; Will. Winstanley, England's Worthies. 1684; Henry Wharton, Anglia Sacra. 1691; James Tyrrel, The General History of England. 1696—1704, — a good translation of Asser; Thomas Birch, The Heads and Characters of Illustrious Persons of Great Britain. 1743 (1751), and James Granger, A Biographical History of England. 1769—74, — both begin in the 16th cent.; Arckenholtz, Annalen der Brittischen Geschichte. 1790; Robert Henry, The History of Great Britain. 12 vols. 1788—95;

Fabyan (d. 1513), sometime sheriff of London, wrote 'The Chronicle
of Fabyan, whiche he hym selfe nameth the concordaunce of historeyes,
nowe newly printed, 7 in many places corrected, as to the dylygent
reader it may apere', which was published in 1542. Here follows the
relevant text (p. 197), — Alfred is in this edition referred to by
Fabyan variously as Aluredus, Alurede, and 'Alured or after some
wryteres Alphred': "It is tolde of hym (Alfred) yᵗ he deuyded yᵉ daye
and nyght in thre partyes, if he were not let by warre or other great
besynes. Whereof. viii. houres he spēt in study and lernyng of scyence,
and other .viii. he spente in prayer and almes dedes with other charytable dedes, 7 other .viii. houres he spente in his naturall reste,
sustinaunce of his body, of the nedes of the realme. The which order
he kept duely by waxen tapers kepte by certayne persons." In 1811
H. Ellis printed the same passage in Fabyan's The New Chronicles of
England and France (p. 170); there are some differences in spelling
only in Ellis's edition.

John Rastell (d. 1536) is the second Tudor chronicler to deal with

---

nor in the French translation of Henry's History, Paris 1788; Sir Francis Palgrave,
The Rise and Progress of the English Commonwealth. 1832; E. A. Freeman, Old
English History. 2nd ed. 1871; J. R. Green, A Short History of the English People.
1874; S. R. Gardiner, A Student's History of England. 1890; J. W. Conybeare,
Alfred in the Chroniclers. 1914; Gilbert Stone, England from the Earliest Times to
the Great Charter. 1916.

Two German historians have been quoted before: J. M. Lappenberg and Reinhold
Pauli. Pauli's work König Aelfred. Berlin 1851, mentions (p. 250) the wax candles
serving as time-measurers, but says nothing about the Alfredian tradition. Neither
does Lappenberg. This German scholar, who, in Heeren and Ukert's Geschichte der
europäischen Staaten, published his painstaking work Geschichte von England, the
first volume of which was printed in Hamburg in 1834, writes (I 341): "Ebenso
gewissenhaft wie seine Einkünfte vertheilte er den Dienst seines Körpers und Geistes
zwischen der Erde und dem Himmel. Zur bessern Benutzung der Nacht und stets
genauen Kunde der flüchtigen Stunden erfand er sich einen Zeitmesser, aus sechs
Lichtern, von denen jedes in einer durch durchsichtige Häute gegen Luftzug ge-
schützten Kapsel vier Stunden brannte (Asser). Und gewiss ist es auch selten einem
Sterblichen gelungen, wie Ælfred, die bessere Hälfte seines irdischen Lebens dem
Höchsten was der Mensch erstreben kann zu weihen, in dem grossen Umfange, wie
es fast nur in zeiten möglich scheint, in welchen die Persönlichkeit des begünstigten
Individuums dem Mechanismus des nachrückenden Zeitalters die anstrebende Bahn
bricht." It seems as if these reflections were inspired by Alfred's threefold division
of the twenty-four hours, but Lappenberg hesitates to mention it. Why? For he
accepted Ingulph!

Alfred's working-day. His work The Pastyme of the ' ople [1529,
p. 298; (ed. Dibdin 1811, p. 127)] records: "This noble k. ˑ Alwrede
deuyded ye nyght and day in .iii. partes, wherof he spent v ˑ howris
in prayer and charytable workis, and other viii howris with his coun-
cellors or in study of scyences, and other viii howris in his naturall
rest and sustinance; which order he kept duly, by tapers of wax
brening, tryeng yᵉ certeynte of yᵉ tyme, except he were let by seknes
or other gret impedimentes." Raphael Holinshed (d. 1580), The Historie
of Englande, London, 1577, p. 218, writes: "But to conclude with this
noble Prince king Alvred, hee was so carefull in his office, that hee
deuided the .xxiiij. houres which contayn the day and night in three
partes, so that eight houres he spent in writing, reding and making his
praiers, other eight hee employed in relieuing his bodye with meate,
drinke, and slepe, and the other .viij. he bestowed in dispatching of
businesse cōcerning the gouernment of the realme. He had in his chapell
a candell of .24. partes whereof euery one lasted an houre: So that the
Sexton to whome that charge was committed by burning of that candell
warned the king euer how the time passed away." Holinshed's Chronicles of England (to 1578), Scotland (to 1571), and Ireland (to 1547),
were first published in 1578; with a continuation to 1586 by John
Hooker alias Vowell, a poet and dramatist (1526—1601); the work was
republished in 1586. In this last edition the same version occurs (p. 149)
in exactly the same words. Holinshed is known to have provided
Shakespeare with the plots for historical tragedies, and there is possibly
one or two veiled allusions in Shakespeare to such a division of the
day as we are discussing here. The learned printer and citizen of
London, John Stow (1525?—1605), also published a Summarie of
Englyshe Chronicles in 1565 as well as The Chronicles of England in
1580 (later called The Annales of England), p. 127: "He deuided the
xxiiij houres of the daye and nighte into three parts: he spent .viij.
houres in writing, reading, & praying: eight in prouision of his body:
& .viij. in hearing and dispatching the matters of his subiects." In a
late issue, that of 1631—32, we find (p. 80) the same phrasing of the
story. The other renowned historian of the day, John Speed (1552?—
1629), also incorporated Malmesbury's statement into The Historie of
Great Britaine in 1611, reprinted in 1632; Booke 71, p. 332: "The day
and night containing twentie foure houres, hee (Alfred) designed
equally to three especiall vses, and then obserued by the burning of a

5

taper set in his Chappel or Oratory; eight houres he spent in contemplation, reading and prayers; eight, in prouision for himselfe, his repose
and health; and the other eight in the affayres of his Common-wealth
and State."

Samuel Daniel (1526—1619), the poet, who also appeared as a
historian: History of England, London 1612, and whose work is
appraised in the Review of English Studies, 1947, pp. 226 ff., also
refers to Alfred (loc. cit. p. 37): "The naturall daie, consisting of 24
howers, he cast into three parts: whereof eight he spent in prayer,
studie and writing: eight in the service of his bodie, and eight in the
affaires of his States. Which spaces (having then no other engine for
it) hee measured by a great waxe light, devided into so many parts,
receaving notice by the keeper thereof, as the severall howres passed
in the burning." John Pits, or Pitseus (1560—1616), a Catholic divine,
published (in Paris) in 1619 Relationum historicarum de rebus Anglicis
tomus primus (no more published); he also refers to "De Alfredo
Magno" (p. 169) and writes: "De eo scriptum legi, quod etiam postquam
Rex esset, ex viginti quatuor horis, quae diem naturalem complent, octo
quotidie scribendo, legendo, & orando consumeret. Atque hac doctrina,
his virtutibus regnum suum ita tractauit, ut tum belli, tum pacis tempore semper floruerit." In 1643 Sir Richard Baker (1568—1645)
published his A Chronicle of the Kings of England, in which Alfred is
highly praised (p. 8): "The virtues of this King, if they were not incredible, they were at least admirable, whereof these may be instances.
The day and night, containing four and twenty hours, he designed
equally to three especial uses, observing them by the burning of a
taper, set in his chapel: (there being at that time, no other way of
distinguishing them). Eight hours he spent in contemplation, Reading
and Prayers: eight in provision for himself, his health and recreation;
and the other eight in the affairs of the Common-Wealth and State."

In 1647 John Milton, the poet, began to write a history of Britain,
but he did not publish it until 1670 under the title of The History of
Great Britain. A second edition was issued in 1671. The edition of
1706 bearing the title of A Complete History of England with the
Lives of all the Kings and Queens thereof ... is the only copy having
been accessible to me. Various scholars write there each their separate
sections of the history, Milton having assigned the first section of the
first volume to himself: "Beginning with the History of Britain to

William the Conqueror". The work is very conscientiously done, the margin informing about the sources, such as Asser, Sax. An., Malmsb., Huntingd., Mat., Mat., Sim. Dun., etc. The passage of interest to us (I 58) runs: "His Time, the Day and Night he distributed by the burning of certain Tapours into three equal Portions: The one was for devotion, the other for publick or private Affairs, the third for bodily Refreshment: How each Hour past, he was put in mind by one who had that office."

Practically all the works mentioned above were reprinted and appeared in several editions. It is clear from the instances given above that in the 17th c. there was a fair knowledge of Alfred the Great's scheme of dividing the natural day into three equal portions.[75a] In the 18th c. this Alfredian tradition was continued. Paul Rapin-Thoyras (1661—1725), a Frenchman, who fled to England in 1686, published his Histoire d'Angleterre in the Hague during 1724—36, of which numerous French editions appeared during the century. At the same time his History was also being published in London in English: The History of England ... "Done into English with additional notes ... by N. Tindal" in 15 volumes during 1725—31. The many editions of it will be found in the chronological table p. 74 below. (The author is not to be confused with René Rapin (d. 1687), the foremost critic of his age in Europe, who became an enormous authority in England and is referred to, for instance, in Fielding's Tom Jones, Bk VI ch. 2, and passim in Sterne's Tristram Shandy.) Rapin-Thoyras was the leading historian in England, until Hume's history ousted him. I quote here from the French edition of 1749; I, p. 321: "Pendant qu'il avoit été caché dans l'Isle d'Athelney, il avoit voué à Dieu de lui consacrer la troisieme partie de son temps, dès qu'il se trouveroit dans un état plus tranquille. Il ne fut pas plutôt parvenu à cet heureux état, qu'il exécuta ponctuellement son voeu, en donnant huit heures

---

[75a] Cf. Louis B. Wright, Middle-Class Culture in Elizabethan England (Chapel Hill, N. C. 1935), ch. IX, s. 297 ff.: 'The Utility of History'. The didactic value of historical studies is confirmed by Tudor and Stuart moralists. Wright says (p. 301): "... middle-class readers especially came to regard history as the perfect literature, for it was safe, entertaining, instructive, and useful . Moreover, a knowledge of national history was an evidence of patriotism ... Therefore historical works of manifold types found their way into the libraries of plain men, who added to their resources of learning by ... reading diligently in the native annals."

par jour aux exercises de piété, huit heures aux affaires publiques, &
autant au sommeil, à l'étude, & à la recréation."

An English historian followed him in the public favour. In 1747
Thomas Carte (1686—1754) published the first volume of A General
History of England. On Alfred he writes among other things (I 304):
"Regularity and economy are generally uniform: and Alfred was the
same good manager of his time, that he was of the revenue. Of the
twenty-four hours of the day, notwithstanding the piles, which plagued
him in a terrible manner from the twentieth to the forty-fifth year of
his age, he assigned only eight to the care of his health, to be spent in
sleep, meals, and exercise: and he employed the other sixteen, one half
in writing, reading, and prayer, the other in dispatching the affairs of
his kingdom. He was so exact in keeping to these proportions and allot-
ments of his time that he measured them by tapers of an equal size;
which were always kept burning before the shrine of the relicks, that
were carried along with him wherever he travelled: and to prevent
their being affected by the wind, or other accidents, he invented horn
lanterns, that he might be sure of their consuming in an equal degree."
Carte quotes William of Malmesbury in various parts of his work.

David Hume (1711—1776), the philosopher, also wrote a History
of England; in 1754 there appeared his history of James I and Charles I, in 1759 the history of the Tudor monarchs, and in 1761 of earlier
epochs. The History of England, pp. 67—68: "But the most effectual
expedient, employed by Alfred, for the encouragement of learning,
was his own example, and the constant assiduity, with which, notwithstanding the multitude and urgency of his affairs, he employed himself
in the pursuits of knowledge. He usually divided his time into three
equal portions; one was employed in sleep, and the refection of his
body by diet and exercise; another in the dispatch of business; a third
in study and devotion: And that he might more exactly measure the
hours, he made use of burning tapers of equal lengths, which he fixed
in lanthorns; an expedient suited to that rude age, when the geometry
of dialling and the mechanism of clocks and watches were totally unknown. (Asser, p. 20. W. Malm. Lib. 2. cap. 4. Ingulf, p. 870. Flor.
Wigorn. p. 594. Chron. Abb. St. Petri de Burgo, p. 22. Anglia Sacra,
vol. i, p. 208.)"

Hume had evidently studied Carte, but perhaps also Asser in
Wise's edition. He adds: "And by such a regular distribution of his

time ... this martiall hero ... was able during a life of no extraordinary length, to acquire more knowledge, and even to compose
more books, than most studious men, though blessed with the greatest
leisure ...." As late as 1818 Mr. Murray published another edition of
Hume's history, where the same statement occurs (I 97): "He usually
divided his time into three equal portions: one was employed in sleep,
and the refection of his body by diet and exercise; another in the
dispatch of business; a third in study and devotion; and that he might
more exactly measure the hours, he made use of burning tapers of equal
length, which he fixed in lanthorns; an expedient suited to that rude
age, when the geometry of dialling, and the mechanism of clocks and
watches were totally unknown." Already the many editions of history
in the eighteenth and nineteenth centuries reassure us that the Alfredian
tradition was common knowledge for a large part of society, —
although this pious story from the 'rude' past did not have any bearing
upon the social life of these centuries. Hume's reflections on the
advisability of adopting Alfred's rule in order to save time and do
more work in the time of our disposal did not aim at reforming the
working hours of the workers and the labourers, which at that time
were increasing; they were only meant as a reminder to the leisured
class that they ought to dispose of their time more efficiently, if they
wished to be well educated.

Next comes John Barrow, a teacher of mathematics to the navy,
about whom very little is known, except the note in D. N. B. (fl. 1756).
He published in 1763—64 A New Impartial History of England ...
in ten volumes, of which there are no copies in the British Museum,
but in the Bibliothèque Nationale in Paris. His work was translated
into French in 1771—73 (10 vols.), Histoire nouvelle et impartiale
d'Angleterre. Since it has not been possible to find the English original,
I quote from the French edition (I 319): "Il (Alfred) partageoit la
journée en trois parties de huit heures chacune; la première pour le
sommeil, les repas et les exercises, la seconde pour la lecture et les
prières, & la troisième pour les affaires publiques. Afin d'éviter toute
confusion ou méprise dans cette distribution, il fit faire six cierges de
douze pouces de longeur & de douce onces. Chacun de ses cierges
brûloit pendant quatre heures." This account is a translation of William of Malmesbury.

In the following year, 1764, there was published anonymously

An History of England, in a series of letters from a Nobleman to his
son; the author proved to be Oliver Goldsmith. In 1771 his History
of England, from the earliest times to the death of George II, was
printed, where Goldsmith again appeared as a historian. It is stated
there: "He (Alfred) usually divided his time into three equal portions;
one was given to sleep, and the refection of his body, diet and exercise;
another to the dispatch of business; and the third to study and devotion." (I 23 in the 1838 ed.) After giving due praise to Alfred seen
from various aspects, Goldsmith, however, ends with a critical note,
more founded on the suspicion that such a perfect man cannot have
existed, than on evidence: "In short, historians have taken such a
delight in describing the hero, that they have totally omitted the
mention of his smaller errors, which doubtless he must have had in
consequence of his humanity." This is a typical 18th c. reflection.
Joseph Strutt (1749—1802) who is best known for his Sports and
Pastimes of the People of England (1801), also wrote a Chronicle of
England, the second volume of which has a reference to the tradition
(II 39, 1778): "When he (Alfred) ascended the throne, that no duties
belonging to his high office might be neglected, he divided each day
into three parts, in which he regularly went through all business whether
public or private."

An indefatigable writer, Alexander Bicknell (d. 1796), whose fancy
had been fired by accounts of Alfred, published in 1788 The Patriot
King, or Alfred and Elvida, an historical tragedy, a tedious version of
Alfred's life with no references to the eight hours' day, but eleven years
earlier, in 1777, he had printed a Life of Alfred the Great, King of
the Anglo-Saxons, where (p. 286) he mentions the rule: "he dedicated
this solemn protestation (i. e. "a vow to set apart for the service of
God the third part of his time" when he lay hid in the Isle of Athelney)
with great punctuality, dedicating eight hours every day to acts of
devotion, eight hours to public affairs, and as many to sleep, study and
necessary refreshments." It is easy to see that Bicknell's source is 'Rapin'.
In the British Museum there is also a single copy of a late 18th c.
history: Charles Allen's A New and Improved History of England,
from the invasion of Julius Caesar to the end of the thirty-second year
of the reign of King George the Third, etc., London 1793. In chapter
III, p. 17, we read: "He (Alfred) usually divided his time into three
equal portions: one was employed in sleep, and the recruiting of his

body by diet and exercise; another in the dispatch of business; and a third in study and devotion. And in order to enable him to measure the hours more exactly, he made use of burning tapers of equal length; for the art of constructing dials, clocks and watches was not then known in England."

Then there is Sharon Turner (1768—1847), the historian, who devoted five volumes of history (1799—1805) to the Old English period: The History of the Anglo-Saxons. A second edition appeared in 1823. Turner is a conscientious historian, and the way in which he deals with the Alfredian time-table is characteristic. Vol. II p. 129, 2nd ed., mentions the division of the day with the help of candles, quite correctly according to Asser, and he continues (p. 130): "Asser's general statement (Asser 67) that he consecrated half his time to God, gives no distinct idea, because we find, that his (Alfred's) liberal mind, in the distribution of his revenue, thought that to apportion money for a school, was devoting it to the Supreme. Malmesbury's account is, that one-third of the natural day and night was given to sleep and refreshment; one-third to the affairs of his kingdom; and one-third to those duties which he considered as sacred. This indistinct statement cannot now be amplified." Turner leaves the question open.

Two other historians were Edmund Burke, the renowned politician and essayist, and Sir James Mackintosh, philosopher, lawyer, and historian. Edmund Burke (1729—1797) has left us in his collected works (Vol. X, 1812 ed., but written in 1757) An Abridgment of English History; from the Invasion of Julius Caesar to the End of the Reign of King John, and there (X 298) he writes about Alfred: "To his religious exercise and studies he devoted a full third part of his time. It is pleasant to trace a genius even in its smallest exertions: in measuring and allotting his time for the variety of business he was engaged in. According to his severe methodical custom, he had a sort of wax candles, made of different colours(!) and different proportions(!) according to the time he allotted to each particular affair; as he carried these about with him wherever he went, to make them burn evenly, he invented horn lanthorns." Burke objects to the practice of attributing to Alfred various institutions, such as shires, hundreds, or tithings: "it is very obvious that the shires were never settled upon any regular plan, nor are they the result of any single design". But he adds that "these reports, however ill-imagined, are a strong proof of the high veneration, in which this excellent prince has been held". James Mackintosh (1765—1832) once opposed Burke on the issue of the French revolution in 1791, but later on they became friends, and when he wrote his History of England in Lardner's Cabinet Cyclopaedia in 1830 (second ed. 1836) he says among other things (I 40): "He (Alfred) devised means of measuring time in order to improve it(!)" and for the rest he follows Asser. He adds (p. 41): ". . . and that it (wars and illness) so little encroached on the duties of government as to leave him for ages the popular model for exact and watchful practice . . . The bright image may long be held up before the national mind. This tradition, however paradoxical the assertion may appear, is in the case of Alfred rather supported than weakened by the fictions which have sprung from it. Although it be an infirmity of every nation to ascribe their institutions to the contrivance of a man rather than to the slow action of time and circumstance, yet the selection of Alfred by the English people as the founder of all that was dear to them is surely the strongest proof of the deep impression left on the minds of all his transcendant wisdom and virtue. — Juries, the division of the island into counties and hundreds, the device of francpledge, the formation of the common or customary law itself, could have been mistakenly attributed to him by nothing less than general reverence."

Burke's account makes it clear that Burke knew about the Alfredian tradition of the three eights, for Asser stated that Alfred devoted half his time to God. Burke's criticism of all the fables attached to the Anglo-Saxon king may well have made him shrink from serving up the old tradition. But why did he mention only one third, and not the two other ones? In Mackintosh the threefold division of the day is wholly left out. But in Mackintosh's as well as in Burke's appreciation of Alfred there is a good deal of enthusiasm, which seems to indicate that if reformers had appealed to the pious king's threefold division of the day in their efforts to bring about more humane conditions for the workmen, their arguments would have carried a good deal of effect. It has always been a characteristic of English political life that agitators for reform should appeal to earlier precedents, as for instance when: ". . . the men who established our civic liberties in the Seventeenth Century appealed to medieval precedents against the 'modernizing' monarchy of the Stuarts." [G. M. Trevelyan, English Social History. (1946, p. 96).]

John Lingard (1771—1851), a Roman Catholic historian, was well-read in Asser; nevertheless he introduces part of the Malmesburian matter. In his work A History of England (8 vol., 1819—1830) he mentions only one third and does not say that the natural day was divided into three equal parts (I p. 193): "In the arrangement of his time, his finances, and his domestic concerns, Alfred was exact and methodical. The officers of his household were divided into three bodies, which succeeded each (p. 194) other in rotation, and departed at the end of the month, the allotted period of their service. (Asser, 65.) Of each day he gave one third to sleep and necessary refreshments: the remainder was divided between the duties of his station, and works of piety and charity. (Malm. 24, 25. Asser, 67). Without the knowledge of chronometers, Alfred was perplexed to discover the true hour of the day. To remedy the inconvenience he had recourse to the following simple expedient. By repeated experiments he found that a quantity of wax, weighing seventy-two denarii, might be made into six candles, each twelve inches long and of equal thickness, and that these, burning in succession, would last exactly 24 hours. To prevent the flame from being affected by currents of air, the candles were inclosed in a large lantern of transparent horn; and as the combustion of each inch of wax corresponded with the lapse of one seventy-second part of the day, or twenty of our minutes, he was hence enabled to measure his time with some accuracy. (Asser, 68, 69.)" Burke chose the religious third of the day, Lingard the third of sleep and refreshment: none of them found any interest in the third of work. Burke had written his Abridgment in 1757, when working hours were not being discussed to any extent. This passing reference may be accidental, but there is the suspicion that Lingard and Mackintosh at least evaded the threefold division on purpose. The first decades of the 19th c. were troublous and quâsi-revolutionary, and the demand for shorter hours became articulated. Are we right to suppose that these two writers deliberately avoided mentioning this tradition among the institutions ascribed to Alfred? The reason might be that they did not wish to drag Alfred's idea of a day's work into the heated discussion about working hours in factories, or perhaps they deliberately refrained from stressing the historic argument for a change in the working hours of labourers and factory workers? However this may be, it is a fact that Southey (Sir Thomas More: or, Colloquies on the Progress and Prospects of Society. 1829.

I 149), when dealing with "The manufacturing System" and the advantages of rising early, also has a mutilated reference to Malmesbury's rule: "They who require eight hours sleep would upon such a system (that is, to rise with the sun all the year round) go to bed at nine during four months." Here again only one third of the Alfredian day is touched upon. Southey was a true friend of Labour in his own conservative way: he did not believe in political measures to relieve the lot of the workers, but tried to inculcate in the rich and the capitalists moral lessons and thus make them relent towards the poor[76]: His Illustrations of the same work (p. 335) refer only to early rising, and nowhere is there to be found any voicing of shorter working hours.

When Charles Dickens wrote his Child's History of England (1851) he had apparently read Turner and Strutt, also Mackintosh, for his version of the tradition runs: "Every day he (Alfred) divided into *certain portions*, and in each portion devoted himself to *a certain pursuit*. (My italics.) That he might divide his time exactly, he had wax torches or candles made, which were all of the same size, were notched across at regular distances, and were always kept burning. Thus, as the candle burnt down, he divided the day into notches, almost as accurately as we now divide it into hours upon the clock." Dickens may have been convinced that the threefold division of Alfred was a spurious invention, but that the time-measurer was a fact, according to Asser. Otherwise the caution with which he avoids

---

[76] (Sir Thomas More): "... But you who neither seek to deceive others nor yourself, ... you who are neither insane nor insincere ... you surely do not expect that the Millennium is to be brought about by the triumph of what are called liberal opinions nor by enabling the whole of the lower classes to read the incentives to vice, impiety and rebellion, which are prepared for them by an unlicensed press; nor by Sunday schools, and Religious Tract Societies; nor by the portentous bibliolatry of the age? — (Montesinos, = Southey's *alter ego*, who first discusses the visions of the Apocalypse, Antichrist, the Beast, etc., but continues): But it leaves my hope unshaken and untouched. I know that the world has improved; I see that it is improving; and I believe that it will continue to improve in natural and certain progress. Good and evil principles are widely at work: a crisis is evidently approaching; it may be dreadful, but I can have no doubts concerning the result. Black and ominous as the aspects may appear, I regard them without dismay. The common exclamation of the poor and the helpless, when they feel themselves oppressed, conveys to my mind the sum of the surest and safest philosophy. I say with them, "God is above", and trust him for the event." (I 35).

mentioning Alfred's rule must be explained as hesitation on the part of the publisher with regard to the threefold division of the day.[77] Similarly in Thomas Hughes's Tom Brown's Schooldays there is an account in the first chapter of the battle of Ashdown and Alfred (taken from Asser through Francis Wise), but there is no mention of Alfred's time division.

In 1840 William of Malmesbury's Chronicle was re-issued by Sir Th. D. Hardy in the English Historical Society Publications. It is true that it was edited in Latin, without a translation, but even so, many Radicals understood Latin. Another foreign language was French, in which language several translations of English histories were published. But it is interesting to find historical works written by Frenchmen with a reference to Alfred's threefold division of the day. There is an Abrégé de l'Historie d'Angleterre, et d'Irlande ... Recueilly de plusieurs Memoires, par Mr M. Historiographe de France (Paris 1652), — who the writer was has not been ascertained. There we read (p. 124): "On tient qu'il fut si bien instruit és bonnes lettres, qu'il escriuit plusieurs liures de son inuention, & en translata d'autres de langue Latine en sa naturelle; & rapporte-on de luy qu'il distribuoit les 24 heures du iour à son vsage, en telle sorte qu'il en employoit huit à mediter, etudier, & composer; autre huit à vaquer aux affaires du Royaume, & le reste à ses commoditez corporelles. Enfin il mourut, apres auoir regné 28 ans."

In 1784 there was published Histoire d'Angleterre I (Paris), which was really only a pictorial book, but every engraving was accompanied by a short account of the scene. The engraver was F. A. David, but the writer has not been identified. He is mentioned only as "l'Auteur", who writes "les Discours". At p. 56 we read: "Son tems étoit aussi distribué en trois portions. Il donnait la première aux affaires de son Royaume, la seconde à l'étude & à ses pieux exercises, le reste aux besoins de la Nature. L'Art de l'Horlogerie n'étoit pas né: son génie y suppléoit, & des flambeaux d'égale longueur mesuroient à ses yeux la succession de ses heures & ses travaux."

---

[77] DICKENS also refers to Alfred's time-measurer in Dombey and Son (Tauchn. ed.; I ch. 14, p. 239): "Paul ... asked him, as a practical man, what he thought about King Alfred's idea of measuring time by the burning of candles; to which the clock-man replied that he thought it would be the ruin of the clock trade if it was to come up again."

That the knowledge of the public with regard to the Alfredian tradition was widespread in the 18th and 19th c. can be taken for granted, and my conviction that the educated classes, politicians generally and Radical reformers, were well aware of it[78] is supported by the following chronological table.

Chronological table of historical works, and new editions of them, containing the Alfredian threefold division of the day.

1480 (Caxton's Epitome of) Polychronicon	1580 Stow	1634 Daniel
	1586 Holinshed	1643 Baker
1482 Caxton's Polychronicon	1596 Savile (Lat.)	1650 Daniel
	1601 Savile (Lat.)	1650 Speed
1495 Wynkyn de Worde's Polychronicon	1611 Speed	1652 Abrégé (French)
	1612 Daniel	1653 Baker
1513 Bradshaw	1613 Daniel	1660 Baker
1527 Treveris's Polychronicon	1616 [Goodwin, Francis], Annales Rerum Anglicarum	1665 Baker
		1670 Milton
1529 Rastell		1670 Baker
1542 Fabyan	1618 Daniel	1673 Maderus (Lat.)
1548 Bale (Lat.)	1619 Pits (Lat.)	1677 Milton
1557 Bale (Lat.)	1623 Daniel	1678 Spelman (Lat.)
1565 Stow	1631 Stow	1678 Milton
1577 Holinshed	1632 Speed	1679 Baker

[78] Cf. W. E. MURPHY, History of the Eight Hours' Movement (Melbourne 1896), an Australian work; Murphy had been secretary of the Eight Hours' Anniversary Committees of Victoria, 1881—3. On p. 4 the writer refers to AUBREY's History of England (1867—70) I p. 73: "He (Alfred) kept in his chapel a wax taper continually burning before the relics of the saints which was divided into equal portions of *eight hours each* ... He also appointed a servant, whose duty it was, as each of these portions was consumed and finished, in a loud voice to warn the king of the portion about to succeed, a wax taper being thus consumed each day." This workman consequently knew the tradition, although only in Aubrey's corrupted version. Murphy continues: "The reference (to the threefold division), therefore, would appear to point to a religious rather than a social origin, and its application to the working hours of the labouring classes is not even suggested by such writers as Dr. Pauli, Hughes, Aubrey, nor Asser ..." He does not believe in an Old English eight hours' day (which, of course, would be sheer nonsense. G. L.), and adds: "... the continued repetition is not a little repugnant to common sense". This is evident, but Murphy, and other critics, such as Webb and Cox (see p. 113 et seq.), did not realize that the Alfredian *tradition* can have played a part when workers began to ask for an 8 hours' day.

1684 Baker	1777 Strutt	1818 Milton
1684 Fulman	1777 Bicknell	1819 Lingard
1685 Daniel	1778 Hume	1819 Goldsmith (twice)
1687 Gale (Lat.)	1779 Strutt	1819 Rapin
1691 Gale (Lat.)	1784 Rapin	1820 Turner
1695 Milton	1784 David (Fr.)	1820 Goldsmith
1696 Baker	1787 Goldsmith	1822 Hume
1706 Milton	1788 Rapin	1823 Turner
1709 Spelman (Hearne)	1788 Goldsmith	1823 Goldsmith
1719 Milton	1788 Hume (Fr.)	1824 Hume
1723 Sparke (Lat.)	1789 Hume	1825 Lingard
1724 Rapin (Fr.)	1790 Hume	1825 Hume
1725 Rapin	1793 Allen	1826 Hume
1730 Baker	1793 Goldsmith	1827 Goldsmith
1732 Rapin	1793 Hume	1828 Goldsmith
1733 Rapin (Fr.)	1794 Goldsmith	1831 Goldsmith (twice)
1733 Baker	1799 Turner	1832 Hume
1736 Rapin (Fr.)	1800 Goldsmith	1833 Lingard (Fr.)
1741 Ludewig (Lat.)	1801 Goldsmith (Fr.)	1834 Hume
1743 Rapin	1802 Hume (twice)	1836 Turner
1745 Otterbourne (Lat.)	1802 Goldsmith	1837 Lingard
1745 Rossi II (Lat.)	1803 Hume	1837 Goldsmith
1747 Carte	1806 Hume	1837 Hume
1747 Rapin	1807 Turner	1837 Goldsmith (Fr.)
1749 Rapin (Fr.)	1807 Hume	1838 Hume
1751 Rapin	1807 Goldsmith (Fr.)	1839 Hume (Fr.)
1757 Burke	1808 Hume	1840 William of Malmes-
1757 Rapin	1811 Hume	bury (Lat. ed.)
1762 Hume	1811 Fabyan (ed.)	1840 Goldsmith
1763 Barrow	1812 Burke	1842 Hume (Span.)
1763 Hume	1812 Goldsmith	1849 Lingard
1770 Hume	1813 Goldsmith	1850 Goldsmith
1771 Barrow (Fr.)	1814 Hume	1851 Dickens
1771 Goldsmith	1816 Hume	1852 Dickens
1773 Hume	1818 Goldsmith	1852 Turner
1774 Goldsmith	1818 Hume (twice)	

Thus, from 1500 to 1850 no less than 140 chronicles, historical works, and text editions were published, 14 of which were in Latin, 12 in French, 1 in Spanish, but the rest, 113 books, in English, — which means that the English reading public was able to read about the Alfredian tradition of dividing the 24 hours into three equal portions every three years. Ever since 1770 until 1850 one book containing the

same device was issued practically every year.[79] Consequently, we
might confidently say that only few learned and well educated people
were ignorant of it; and many of the workers, esp. the Reformers
generally, must have known it. This does not mean that even Reformers applied it at once to practical politics; but evidently the Alfredian
division of the 24 hours of the day seemed to be an ideal solution to
those interested in working conditions. To say that only fragmentarv
knowledge of the Alfredian tradition in this sense prevailed at about
1800 and later is obviously erroneous.

V.

Apart from the chroniclers and historians and their treatment of the
Alfredian tradition, there are countless references in literature during
the course of the centuries to what is considered the best way of dividing one's time.

Already in Chaucer, in the Shipman's Tale, we meet a prescription
for hours of sleep (l. 125 ff.). The merchant's wife and the friar Daun
John meet in the garden early in the morning, and when the wife
expresses her surprise that Daun John is up so early, he replies that it is
sufficient to sleep five hours; only old wights, as are married men, like
to doze. Chaucer returns to the dangers of long sleep in the Parson's
Tale (§ 82): "Slepinge longe in quiete is eek a greet norice (nurse) to
Lecherie." The same idea is found in Burton's Anatomy of Melancholy,
(ed. 1891, p. 356): "Seven or eight hours is a competent time for a
melancholy man to rest, as Crato thinks; but as some do, to lie in bed
and not sleep, a day, or half a day together, to give assent to pleasing
conceits and vain imaginations, is in many ways pernicious."; and in
the well-known first stanza of The Sluggard by Isaac Watts (1674—
1748): "'Tis the voice of the sluggard; I heard him complain, 'You
have wak'd me too soon, I must slumber again'." Andrew Borde, the
Tudor physician, is more serious in his prescription of sleep in A Com-
pendious Regyment or a Dyetary of helth (1557; Elizabethan Prose,
ed. Michael Roberts. 1933. p. 32): "Olde Auncyent Doctors of physicke

---

[79] It is even possible that what THOMAS GRAY called "sixpenny" histories of
England, "by way of question and answer, for the use of children" (Gray's letter to
Beattie, Feb. 1, 1768) also included the Alfredian tradition. I have not been able to
track any of them, however.

sayth. viii. howres of slepe in sommer, and .ix. in wynter, is suffyent for any man: but I do thynke that slepe oughte to be taken as the complexion of man is." François Rabelais, the French doctor and writer, gives to a monk the memorable words, "Les heures sont faictez pour l'homme, et non l'homme pour les heures" (The hours are made for Man, and not Man for the hours; Gargantua, Book I ch. 41), and in Pantagruel (Book IV ch. 64) he quotes "doctors, who explain the canonical hour to be, Rise at five, dine at nine, Sup at five, bed at nine", quoted by J. Hampson, The English at Table (1946. p. 13), while Bilfinger (Die antiken Horen p. 93) gives another version: "lever à six, dîner à dix / souper à six, coucher à dix / nous fait vivre dix fois dix". There seems to be an echo of this in one (No 46) of the Proverbs of Hell in The Marriage of Heaven and Hell by William Blake (1793): "Think in the morning. Act in the noon, Eat in the evening. Sleep in the night." In Lord Lytton's novel Paul Clifford (1830), a highwayman sings a song in praise of the free life of a robber (p. 129): "Rise at six, / dine at two / Rob your men without ado . . ."

Sheavyn[80] has calculated that the Elizabethan grammar school hours averaged from seven to eight hours a day. Comenius, the Czech pedagogue, must have seemed very revolutionary to his contemporaries when he suggested that "the teaching should not be tiring, but as easy as possible. Only four hours a day ought to be devoted to public lessons." And he adds, remarkably enough: "The natural day has twenty-four hours. If for the purpose of employing them in the service of Life we divide them into three portions, eight go to sleep, just as much can be devoted to exterior business (such as the care of one's health, meals, dressing and undressing, rest, honourable amusements, meeting friends, etc.), while there still remain eight hours for serious work, which, however, has to be done with joy and without aversion. Every week will consequently contain forty-eight working hours — each seventh day is devoted wholly to rest, — every year 2,495; — how much then in a space of 10, 20, 30 years?" Comenius expresses his ideas in Didactica Magna of 1657.[81] There is no doubt that Comenius got this idea ulti-

---

[80] PH. SHEAVYN, The Literary Profession in the Elizabethan Age. Manchester 1909, p. 116.

[81] COMENIUS, Didactica Magna. cap. 15, item 16, col. 70 (ed. Opera Didactica Omnia, 1657): "Dies naturalis horas habet viginti quatuor: quibus ad vitæ usum *tripartito divisio, octo cedent somno; totidem externis negotiio,* (Valetudini puta

mately from William of Malmesbury.[82] Speaking of schools it may be
of interest to note what a Swedish scholar, Samuel Columbus, scribbled
down in verse in his diary when in Paris in 1677, about the day of a
university student: "Seven hours to sleep, / One hour to praise God, /
Seven hours to read (sc. study), / One hour to refresh one's nose, / Two
hours for meals, / Two hours to forget all sorrow, / The other four you
may take as they come, / With gossip and drinking, but careful and
pious, though."[83]

It is told of St. Bridget, the medieval Swedish saint, that she ad-
monished King Magnus of Sweden, saying that the Evil One had told
him to devote nineteen hours of twenty to amusements and only one
to God! This story has not been verified. A regular division of hours
seems to have been popular in early times although Malmesbury's threefold measurement of the day was unique. When we meet the Constable's
reflection in Middleton's The Mayor of Queenborough (I 1; Dyce's ed.
p. 136, 1839): "Eight hours a-day in serious contemplation / Is but a
bare allowance; no higher food / To the soul than bread and water to
the body; / And that's but needful, when more would do better ...",
there is no doubt concerning the source of the saying, especially as
"Raynulph" (Higden), Monk of Chester, appears as 'Induction' and

curandæ, funiendo cibo, induendis & exuendis vestibus, recreationi honestæ, amico-
rum confabulationibus &c) *seriis denique laboribus, alacriter jam & sine tædio ex-
pediundis, superient octo.* Hebdomativa itaque (die septimo quiete relicto integre)
habebuntur operis destinandæ horæ 48; annuatim 2495: qvid autem non intra decem,
viginti, triginta, annos?" — This applies apparently to the adults; for schoolchildren
Comenius has another prescription; ibid. Cap. XII. (VI, col. 53. ed. Opera Didactica
omnia, 1657): "Ut formatura hæc non operosa sit, sed facillima: nempe non nisi
quatuor horas quotidie tribuendo publicis exercitiis; & quidem ita, ut Præceptor
unicus vel centenis simul erudiendis sufficiat, decuplô faciliore operâ, quàm quanta
nunc in singulos impendi solet." — Nothing about this in ROBERT FITZGIBBON YOUNG,
Comenius in England. Oxford 1932.

[82] BETSY RODGERS, Cloak of Charity. London 1949, p. 102, gives the time-table
of the pious Robert Raikes's Sunday school for poor children in Gloucester in 1784:
"It was ordered that the children should attend from 8 till 10.30 in the morning,
and then go to morning service; that they should go to church again in the afternoon, and return to school from 5.30 till 8 in the evening — more or less a twelve-
hour day of devotion." And 8 hours to attend divine service.

[83] SAMUEL COLUMBUS, MS. Book Uppsala Univ. Libr. Hs. V. 301, p. 146 f., where
there are two versions. Columbus's hand is rather difficult to read in certain places,
owing to crossings and alterations. I agree, however, with RAGNAR EKHOLM, Samuel
Columbus. Uppsala 1924, p. 12.

'Chorus' in the play. Higden was the chronicler who most of all spread the Alfredian tradition. To me a passage in Shakespeare's 3 H VI is a paraphrase on Malmesbury's division of the day (II v. 21 ff.):

> O God! methinks it were a happy life,
> To be no better than a homely swain;
> To sit upon a hill, as I do now,
> To carve out dials quaintly, point by point,
> Thereby to see the minutes how they run,
> How many make the hour full complete;
> How many hours bring about the day;
> How many days will finish up the year;
> How many years a mortal man may live.
> When this is known, then to divide the times:
> So many hours must I tend my flock;
> So many hours must I take my rest;
> So many hours must I contemplate;
> So many hours must I sport myself; . . .

It is true that The True Tragedie of Richard Duke of York, and the Death of Good King Henrie the Sixt (London 1595) does not include King Henry's reflections on the shepherd's life, and that Robertson, Marlowe (1931, p. 95), points out that Fleay has found a parallel in Drayton's The Legend of Robert Duke of Normandy (stanza 93), but the latter writes only six similar lines beginning: "So many years as he had worn a crown, So many years as he had hoped to rise . . ." The division of the day in definite portions for definite occupations makes it probable that Shakespeare was influenced by Malmesbury — or Higden, viâ Holinshed. Wolsey's words in his Henry VIII. III. 2. 144 f. have also some affinity:

> For holy offices I have a time; a time
> To think upon the part of business which
> I bear i' the state; and nature does require
> Her times of preservation . . .,

just as Bishop Gardiner's (ibid. I 1. 2 f.):

> These should be hours for necessities,
> Not for delights; times to repair our nature
> With comforting repose, and not for us
> To waste these times.

6

Sir Edward Coke, the famous lawyer, (1552—1634) has a Latin distich, the translation of which runs: "Six hours in sleep, in law's grave study six, / Four spend in prayer, the rest on Nature fix." In John Wilson Croker's edition of Boswell's Life of Dr. Johnson (V 233) Croker drags in a modified version of this by Sir William Jones, the Oriental scholar, and points out the discrepancy that Jones apparently counted only twenty-three hours of a natural day. This edition of Johnson's Life met with a severe criticism by Lord Macaulay; inter alia he also touches upon Croker's inability to understand the passage.

"All our readers have doubtless seen the two distichs of Sir William Jones, respecting the division of the time of a lawyer. One of the distichs is translated from some old Latin lines; the other is original. The former runs thus: —

'Six hours to sleep, to law's grave study six,
Four spend in prayer, the rest on nature fix.'

'Rather', says Sir William Jones,

'Six hours to law, to soothing slumbers seven.
Ten to the world allot, and all to heaven.'

The second couplet puzzles Mr. Croker strangely. 'Sir William' says he, 'has shortened his day to twenty-three hours, and general advice of 'all to heaven' destroys the peculiar appropriation of a certain period to religious exercises.'

"Now, we did not think that it was in human dullness to miss the meaning of the lines so completely. Sir William distributes twenty-three hours among various employments. One hour is thus left for devotion. The reader expects that the verse will end with 'and one to heaven'. The whole point of the lines consists in the unexpected substitution of 'all' for 'one'. The conceit is wretched enough, but it is perfectly intelligible, and never, we will venture to say, perplexed man, woman or child before." (Critical and Historical Essays. ed. 1886, I 172.) Lord Macaulay, it seems, must have been in a very scathing mood when he criticised poor Croker on this very point; the counting is weak and Macaulay's explanation is not much better. A correspondence in the English press has elicited the following variants of Jones's couplet.

a) Eight hours to work   b) Eight hours for sleep,
   To pleasing slumbers seven;   Eight hours for prayer,
   Nine to the world allot,   Eight hours for work,
   And all to Heaven.   And all to the Glory of God.

In the last couplet the Alfredian tradition has crept in; both are
relative recent. As to office hours for lawyers and statesmen it may
be pointed out that Axel Oxenstierna ("Oxenstern"), a Swedish statesman of the 17th c., made it a rule to get up at 4 o'clock, and to be in
the chancery at 7, — the others had begun work at 6. On Wednesdays
and Fridays, however, everybody began work at 8; on Saturdays there
was no work. There was a break for dinner of four hours every day,
and the office was shut at 5 p.m., so, on three days of the week, the
civil servants worked 7 hours; on the other two only 4 or 5 hours.[84]
To judge from Pepys's Diary (1660—69) no definite office hours were
kept and the day's work was an elusive quantity.[85] In his essay on
Warren Hastings (Oct. 1841) Macaulay estimates the regular sessions
of a court at 9 hours a day (Critical and Historical Essays, ed. 1886,
II 652): "A well constituted tribunal, sitting regularly six days in the
week, and nine hours in the day, would have brought the trial of
Hastings to a close in less than three months." Sir John Sloane, the
architect to the Bank of England for 45 years, used to work between
7 and 7 in the summer and 8 and 8 in the winter(!).[86] Christian August
Gottlieb Gæde, who visited England in 1802—3, relates in his book
England och Wales (Stockholm 1814; IV 66) that the learned men in
England as a rule kept a working-day of 8 hours, from 8 a.m. to 4 p.m.
In Little Dorrit (1855), Bk I ch. 5, Dickens gives Clennam business
hours from 10 to 6, "allowing for intervals of invalid regimen of

---

[84] NILS AHNLUND, Axel Oxenstierna. 1940 p. 340.

[85] The office hours in East India House are given in a verse parody, said to be
by Peacock (Early Victorian England, ed. G. M. YOUNG, 1934, I p. 401):

> From 10 to 11 ate a breakfast for seven;
> From 11 to noon to begin 'twas too soon;
> From 12 to 1 asked 'What's to be done?'
> From 1 to 2 found nothing to do;
> From 2 to 3, began to foresee
> That from 3 to 4 would be a damn bore.

[86] QUENNELL, M. and C. H. B., A History of Everyday Things in England ...
1733—1851. 1933 p. 159.

oysters and partridges", and in the same chapter Little Dorrit herself
worked with her needle from eight to eight. "What became of Little
Dorrit between the two eights was a mystery." We must certainly
conceive Thackeray's minute description of his daily work as editor of
a magazine, the Cornhill, to be a satire upon the discussions about the
advantages and the drawbacks of a reduction of factory hours (in
Round-about Papers; 1861—2): "Intellectual labour sixteen hours;
meals, thirty-two minutes; exercise, a hundred and forty-eight minutes;
conversation with the family, chiefly literary, and about the house-
keeping, one hour and four minutes; sleep, three hours and fifteen
minutes (at the end of the month, when the Magazine is complete, I
own I take eight minutes more); and the rest for the toilette and the
world."
　　　　　　　　　　*　　　　　*
　　　　　　　　　　　*

The regulations governing the working hours of labourers and craftsmen in the Act of 1495 were to last for several centuries. They were
re-enacted in various later statutes. In 6 Hen VIII (1514—15) c. 4 the
same length of working hours is prescribed, and also in 5 Eliz 1562—3,
c. 4: "And be it ... That all artificers and labourers, being hired for
wages by the day or week shall, between the midst of the months of
march and september, be and continue at or before 5 o'clock a.m. at
their work, and not depart until betwixt six and eight o'clock at night,
except it be in the time of breakfast, dinner and drinking, the which
times at the most shall not exceed two hours and a half in the day,
that is to say at every drinking one half hour, for his dinner one hour,
and for his sleep, when he is allowed to sleep, which is from the midst
of may to the midst of august, half an hour at the most, and at every
breakfast one half hour.[87] And all the said artificers, between the midst
of september and the midst of march, shall be and continue at their
work from the spring of the day in the morning, until the night of the
same day, except it be in time before appointed for breakfast and dinner, upon pain to lose and forfeit one penny for every hour's absence,
to be deducted and defaulked out of his wages, that shall so offend."[88]

---

[87] A half-hour is thus added to the 2 hours for the workmen's meals in
11 Hen VII.
[88] STEFFEN's (I 425) English quotation is incomplete. — Cf. Burgh Rec. Stirling,
I 35. 1529 (1887) — see NED sub *night* v. 1 b. = to cease work at night: Till

In the preamble of Elizabeth's act it is said that regard has been taken to the higher prices which cannot be applied "conveniently without the great greefe and burden of the poore labourer and hired men". All the previous acts are now brought together into one, and the intention was to "banishe idlenes advance husbandrye and yeelde unto the hired persone bothe in the tyme of scarsitee and in the tyme of plentye a convenient proporcion of wages". But the employed were to be engaged for at least a whole year; if a labourer was not to his master's liking, he should have a quarter's warning. Unmarried persons were to be forced to work, and persons between twelve and sixty were required to work in husbandry. This was a change for the worse, for 6 Hen VIII (1514—15) laid down that no children "with image (within age? G. L.) of fourteen years" should work. We shall presently see how the custom changed in this respect. Further, Elizabeth prescribed fines for employers who discharged their workmen, and for workers a term of imprisonment if they would not agree to complete their service. No workman could leave the parish, borough or town, without a licence.

The medieval type of working day remained. Nobody thought a shorter day was desirable or practicable; the workers were more concerned with higher wages and personal liberty; Caliban's joyful shouts (Tempest II 2 194): "Freedom, hey-day! Hey-day, freedom!" were heartily shared by other bondmen. The working hours were thus twelve each day even in Elizabethan times. But Thorold Rogers insists again that in practice the workmen did about eight hours in those days,[89]

---

entyr to his werk at day lycht in the morwyng, laif at half hour to twelf at none, and nycht at ewyn.

[89] The administrative machinery of highway repairs was unsatisfactory, which appears in the statute 2 and 3 Ph. & M. c. 1. To remedy this four days' roadwork was requested from every labourer in the parish. Every owner of a carve of land, pasture, or cart had to be at the place appointed with the men upon pain of paying ten shillings a day, and every householder, cottager, and labourer, not being hired servants, had also to contribute *eight hours' labour* for a similar period. — But this did not apply to one day. An early instance of an 8 hours' day is alleged to be found in a French statute. I found it in a French newspaper of about 30 years ago, but I have not been able to verify the statement. The regulation is said to have been issued in 1579 for miners in Burgundy: "the workmen are to work 8 hours a day in the mines: the work divided into two shifts of 4 hours each. If it is necessary to hurry, the work must be carried on by 4 workmen, who have to work 6 hours each in turn without ceasing, in such a way that after 6 hours one worker hands on his tools to the next comer, and then enjoys a rest of 18 hours.

although he admits that the situation grew worse after 1563. "I contend
that from 1563 to 1824, a conspiracy, concocted by the law and carried
out by parties interested in its success, was entered into, to cheat the
English workman of his wages, to tie him to the soil, to deprive him
of hope, and to degrade him into irremediable poverty." (p. 398). Some
of these conjectures of Rogers seem substantial: even 5 Eliz 1562—3
represents a worsening with regard to children's work and the mobility
of labour. Cunningham writes (p. 523), that the statute of 1549 forbade the workmen, by taking oaths, to agree that they will not work

---

The miners should be paid according to agreement with the mine management or
by piece-work, just as they wish. On Holy days accepted by the state the worker
shall be paid just as if he had worked. At Easter, Christmas and Whitsun only
half a week's work is required, except for the boys who are busy pumping out the
water to prevent the flooding of the mines. On the four Virgin Mary holidays and
the twelve Apostle days the worker is free after half a day's work. The miners are
entitled to choose sites for building their own houses and plant their own gardens on
commons where they work and they have the right to pick wood for fuel there."
Some of these regulations make the statute seem spurious.

On the other hand, there are instances of a much harder day's work in at least
one gild in Sweden, that of the saddlers and harness-makers (before 1437). There
the regulation is that: "Any apprentice working for wages must work till the
clock strikes 9 in the evening, and rise when the clock strikes 3 in the morning.
Whoever is late according to what is here prescribed has lost that day (i. e. he receives
no payment). Apprentices serving for wages must work by candlelight fourteen days
before Michaelmas and fourteen days after Lent." (See G. E. KLEMMING, Skrå-
ordningar. Svenska Fornskriftsällskapet 27. p. 6.)

The regulations of the English guilds as represented in English Gilds (EETS orig.
ser. 40) do not contain, as far as I have been able to check them, any regulations
regarding working hours. The one exception is the Gild of Fullers of Bristol, in
1496 (ibid. p. 285): "And moreover, the said servants shall work and rest in their
craft, as well by night as by day, all the year as has of old time been accustomed."
However the gilds whose regulations are quoted are mostly religious brotherhoods
and apparently associations of masters.

As to children's work, one Swedish gild (that of the Shoemakers, before 1474;
see Klemming above) prescribes that (p. 18): "A boy who is twelve years old, may
be on trial for a month" to see if he is suitable; a boy who is 15 years old, may be
on trial for a fortnight.

For Elizabethan apprentices see CAMP pp. 2, 4, 9, 10, 31. In 5 Eliz (1562—63)
children are forced to serve from the age of 12 years (to 60); beggars over 14 years
shall be imprisoned till next session; and in 14 Eliz (1572) rogues of the same age be
put in the stocks. Apparently the fourteenth year was the threshold of adult life:
the same act, 14 Eliz (1572), c. xxiv, states that "beggars' children from five to
fourteen years may be bound to work."

except for a certain payment, and that they will not work overtime, i. e. outside the working-hours prescribed; and (p. 535) that the working hours of 6 Hen VIII were identical with those of 11 Hen VII, and the statute of 1549 forbade only the inevitable consequence of 11 Hen VII and 6 Hen VIII, in that labourers and artisans, by agreement, refused to work overtime. — It is clear that in the Late Middle Ages some labourers and artisans wanted to get fixed working hours, and found Hen VII's and Hen VIII's too long. Further, Cunningham writes (p. 535, footnote 5): "Professor Thorold Rogers speaks of these hours (for the Act of 1514 is almost identical with that of 1495, and follows it in the important section, where it prescribes the exact hours of labour) as prescribed by an act of Elizabeth (Six Centuries 542), and apparently regards it as part of the supposed conspiracy on the part of Parliament and the justices to depress the condition of the labourer. But the Act of Elizabeth merely repeats the regulation as to hours which had already appeared in 1514 and 1495: a clause thus repeated probably embodied the ordinary custom, especially as it was introduced in an Act, the provisions of which about wages fairly correspond with ordinary custom.

"The grounds on which Professor Rogers infers from various industrial indications that the working day only lasted eight hours, are very slight. His chief point is that payments were made for extra hours, amounting to 48 hours a week, and he argues that the normal day must have been short to allow of eight hours a day overtime. Is it impossible that this payment was for the united overtime of a gang of several men, not for the extra work done by a single man?" The regulations as to hours were no doubt harsh and severe. But we have always to reckon with the human factor: some employers would observe the letter of the law if it suited them while others would ignore it. It is interesting to compare these regulations with those applying to gipsies. In 22 Hen VIII 1530—31, "an acte concerning Egypsyans, people callyng themselfes Egyptians", it was prescribed "that from henceforth no such people be suffered to come within this kinges realm"; those who were there already had to leave the country upon pain of losing their possessions; any goods they had were to be restored to parties robbed. The gipsies stayed, however, and 1 and 2 Phil and Mary c. 4 (1554—55) recited the regulations: gipsies were reckoned as felons and fines were increased. But they stayed on. — 5 Eliz c. 20 1562—63 prescribed punishments of "Vagabondes callyng themselves Egiptians",

but those who were born within the country were allowed to remain in
the country. The gipsies had won. This is illustrative of the inefficiency
of the Tudor laws. — One is reminded of Massinger's words (A New
Way to pay Old Debts, V 1): "Which is the reason that the politic /
And cunning statesman, that believes he fathoms / The counsels of all
kingdoms on the earth, / Is by simplicity oft over-reached?" Cf. also
Dekker, The Bellman of London (1608) (in Judges, Elizabethan Under-
world s. 307).

It seems as if the stipulations of the acts were not always observed.
"I know, said Margaret, that this summer (and especially against these
holi-daies) you will worke till ten, and I promise you by eleven I will
have as good a posset for you as ever you did taste on ..." This is
said about a shoemaker c. 1600; cf. Deloney, Gentle Craft II, ed. Mann.
p. 149. In Middleton's play Michaelmas Term (1607) there is a dialogue
(III 1) between a Country Wench and a Tailor: "Why do you work
a Sundays, tailor?" — "Hardest of all a Sundays, because we are most
forbidden." The ban on Sunday work continued, but in some trades the
employers chose not to observe it. So in Hamlet (I l. 76): "Why such
impresse of Shipwrights whose sore Taske, Do's not diuide the Sunday
from the weeke."

Markham's Farewell to Husbandry (4th ed. 1649) records that even
in the month of January a ploughman ought not to rise later than
4 a.m. to get ready for work. He has half an hour for breakfast and
then begins work at 7 a.m. sharp. Work lasts until 2 or 3 p.m., and
another meal is served. After that meal he is busy with the cows, or
sheep. At 6 o'clock supper, and then busy until 8 p.m. with indoor
work: mending shoes and tools, preparing hemp, and brewing of malt
.cider. Then a visit to the stable, and finally to bed — to wake up again
before 4 a.m. This makes a working day of 16 hours, of which 7 to 8
hours are taken up in ploughing in winter. Markham finds this an ideal
working day that ought to obtain everywhere.

John Rae, Eight Hours for Work, London 1894, p. 4, seems to have
a rosier view of Markham's working-day. His book was written as
propaganda for the eight hours' day; hence he is anxious to find earlier
instances of this custom.[90] I have been able to check all Rae's state-

---

[90] I regret that I have to interrupt the chronological description of the working
hours by giving so much space to the refutation of Rae's arguments. But it is neces-

ments, and in Markham's instance he writes: "If Gervase Markham in his Farewell to Husbandry (ed. 1668, p. 112) is describing the common practice, and not laying down a model merely, field work in the seventeenth century occupied 7 or 8 hours without a break, beginning at seven in the morning, and ending at 2 or 3 in the afternoon. Besides that, the servants had stable work in the morning, for which, inclusive of time for prayers he allows two hours; they had to feed the horses at 4 and 8, prepare their fodder for next day, water them, and when not otherwise engaged in the evening, they might be mending shoes for themselves or the master's family, or picking apples or candle rushes, or beating flax. These would seem to be rather devices to occupy spare time than part of their obligatory task; and on the whole there seems little doubt that Hodge led a much easier life in the reign of Elizabeth than he leads now in the greater reign of Victoria."

I will not try to dispute Rae's reflection on the difference between the Elizabethan and the Victorian epochs. But his attitude to the lesser tasks which the servants did late in the day is rather misleading. For Rae field work was the only job worth mentioning; all the other odds and ends of work did not interest him. Now, I have had to work in Sweden as a railway official in 1910 for eight hours a day. Work began at 6.30 with a break at 8.15; I began again at 9, and worked until 10; began at 10.45, break at 11.30; began at 2, break at 3.30; began at 4.30, break at 6; began at 7, stopped at 8.30. This was, of course, a parody on 8 working hours. How much were the breaks worth? According to statistics I had worked only eight hours, but the whole day was spoilt and I was scarcely able to do anything else but see to it, that I was at my job at the right time. This timetable lasted for one year.

One ought perhaps to examine Rae's other statements. On the very first page of his interesting book he says: "Adam Smith in the Wealth of Nations (no reference) speaks as if 8 hours a day were then the usual time of work among colliers, and the statement is confirmed by the explicit statement of Gabriel Jars, a mining engineer who visited the English and Scotch mines about the year 1765, and mentions that the Scotch miners wrought in two shifts of 7 or 8 hours each, and the

---

sary to 'debunk' them since his opinions apparently weighed heavily in the debate on working hours some fifty years ago.

Newcastle miners in two shifts or 6 or 7 hours each." Rae probably
refers to Book I of the Wealth of Nations, Chapter X, Part I (in
Edwin Cannan's ed. 1904 p. 102), where Part I has the heading: "In-
equality arising from the Nature of the Employments themselves."
Smith writes there: "First, The Wages of labour vary with the ease or
hardship, the cleanliness or dirtiness, the honourableness or dishonour-
ableness of the employment. Thus in most places take the year round, a
journeyman taylor earns less than a journeyman weaver. His work is
much easier. A journeyman weaver earns less than a journeyman smith.
His work is not always easier, but it is much cleanlier. *A journeyman
blacksmith, though an artificer, seldom earns so much in twelve as a
collier, who is only a labourer, does in eight.* (Italics mine.) His work
is not quite so dirty, is less dangerous, and is carried on in day-light,
and above ground ... The trade of a butcher is a brutal and an odious
business; but it is in most places more profitable than the greater part
of common trades. The most detestable of all employments, that of
public executioner, is, in proportion to the quantity of work done, better
paid than any common trade whatever." If we take this to mean that
the collier worked only eight hours a day — although this is a comparison of wages per hour, not of working time, — then the blacksmith worked 12 hours, not eight! (See the italicized lines!).

In Jars's work one finds most correctly the reference I 320, which
(dealing with Newcastle miners) runs: "Die Bergleute arbeiten fast
durchgängig in Gedinge (payment by the job), welches nach der Mäch-
tigkeit der Kohlenflötze verschieden ist ... Die Bergleute fahren ge-
meiniglich früh morgens um 2 Uhr, in Begleitung des Bergmeisters an,
der ihnen die Arbeit anweiset, und sie halten täglich nur eine Schicht
von 6 bis 7 Stunden." Consequently Rae had rendered this passage
rightly. But he does not mention the most important additional lines:
"Ausser denen Hauern giebt es noch viele kleine Jungen, welche von
früh morgens um 2 Uhr bis Nachmittags um 4 Uhr in der Grube bleiben,
in welcher Zeit sie die Kohlenkübel füllen ... Es ist übrigens diese
Grube des bösen Wetters wegen ... sehr gefährlich." In his zeal to prove
that the colliers worked an 8-hour day, Rae overlooked the passage
where Jars mentions child labour in the mines as lasting 14 hours a day!
If we turn to Part II of Jars's work (II 438) we find the following
about Scottish miners in 1765: "Die Arbeit auf diesen und auf den
übrigen Flötzen geschieht in Gedinge. Die Gedinghauer (in the French

original maîtres ouvriers qu'on nomme Entrepreneurs, not to be rendered by the German Steiger, says the translator) machen Kameradschaften aus, sie müssen sich das Gezähe und das Geleuchte selbst halten ... und halten täglich doch nur eine Schicht von 7 bis 8 Stunden." The earliest morning shift requires work in a creeping position. — It is evident that the work as a coal cutter was so tiring that the masters did not think it would pay to keep the miners working longer hours, and, besides, the rule was payment by the job. Rae's conclusions on the works quoted were not too reliable. Neither is his conclusion drawn from a passage out of Arthur Young's A Six Months Tour through the North of England (II 288, in ed. London 1770; according to Rae II 262) where he mentions the miners of Mr. Danby's little coal mine at Swinton: "Miners in general, I might almost say universally, are a most tumultuous sturdy set of people, greatly impatient of controul, very insolent, and much void of common industry. Those employed in the lead mines of Craven and in many collieries, can scarcely, by any means, be kept to the performance of a regular business; upon the least disgust, they quit their service, and try another. No bribes can tempt them to any industry after the first performance of their stated work, which leaves them half the day for idleness, or rioting at the alehouse." It is this "half the day" that provokes Rae's idea that they worked — or were allowed to work — about 8 hours. But Young's words are that they cannot be forced to work longer than they want, or they will quit. A collier's job was, of course, a very fatiguing and dangerous one in those days, especially in a lead mine. Besides, Young (and Rae) quotes the case of the old miner who had been allowed to cultivate a few acres of a moor, and Young says himself (p. 298): "The regular severe fatigue of *12 hours* labour in the colliery has not been sufficient to bow down the spirit of this poor fellow; — he applies the remainder of the day, and even steals from the night, to prosecute his favourite works of husbandry — that is, to make up his hours of work TWENTY, out of twenty-four."

Another of Rae's sources is Marshall's Review of Reports to the Board of Agriculture for the Midland Department of England (1815). Marshall's Review is actually made up of extracts from another report, entitled General View of the Agriculture of the County of Bedford, drawn up by order of the Board of Agriculture and Internal Improvement, by Thomas Batchelor, Farmer, 1808. It is quite clear that

Marshall has nothing but contempt for Mr. ·Batchelor, and doubts his qualifications for making such a report. I quote from Marshall's preface (p. 565): "Mr. Batchelor, it is obvious, naturally possesses a considerable compass of mind. But his attainments would seem to be those of a man of general reading, and an amateur of science, rather than those of a practical husbandman, an acquirement which is doubtless intended to be conveyed by the addition 'Farmer'." Nor does Marshall think very highly of Batchelor's methods of collecting information, as he seems to have relied to a great extent upon second-hand sources. However, even if we take it that the information is fairly sound, a different interpretation from the one favoured by Rae may be drawn from this passage. I quote in full from pages 588—9: "Workpeople: — The greatest part of the business of husbandry is performed by day labourers in every part of the county. It is common, however, on most farms of considerable size, to retain annual servants in the capacity of horse-keeper, cowman, shepherd and kitchen-maid, though the great advance in the price of provisions has apparently contributed to diminish the number of domestic servants of every description. It seems generally agreed that the horse-keeper ought to attend the horses at 4 o'clock in the morning, to allow them a sufficient time to feed, and get them properly geared for their work before he takes his breakfast. The team is taken to work as soon as it is light in the winter; at six o'clock or the time when the labourers come, in the spring; and about five, or as soon as convenient, in harvest. About ten o'clock, an interval of a quarter of an hour or more is allowed for the servants to feed. This is called 'beaver-time'; but when the business of ploughing is performed by the labourers, who have no mess in the house with the servants, they sometimes delay their breakfast till nine, which generally occupies half-an-hour. It is common to finish ploughing from one to two o'clock. The horse-keeper attends his horse in the afternoon, and frequently does not entirely leave them for the night till eight o'clock." Now it seems to me that although Rae is correct to say that ploughing takes place from 6 a.m. to 1 or 2 p.m., he overlooks the fact that in many (if not most) cases the horse-keeper and the ploughman are one and the same person, giving him working hours from 4 a.m to 8 p.m. — quite a different matter!

The full passage referred to by Rae as it stands in Marshall's Rural Economy of Norfolk (London 1787) is as follows (I 138): "The universal practice, I believe throughout the county, is to get what is called two journeys. In winter, when days are short, the teams go out as soon as it is light, and return home at twelve o'clock to dinner; go out again at one, and remain in the fields until dark. In longer days the custom varies; the most general practice is to go out at seven in the morning, return at noon, go out again at two, and return at seven in the evening. Ten hours — namely, five hours each journey, are the longest hours of work, except in the hurry of barley-seed time, when these hours may sometimes be exceeded. The length of day is, therefore, not excessive, but the work performed in so short a time is extraordinary. The Norfolk ploughmen always do as much — in general a great deal more — in one journey, that is five hours — than ploughmen in general do in eight hours; which, in most parts of the kingdom, is the length of the ploughman's day. This fact, however, is no longer extraordinary, when we observe their paces respectively. Plough teams in general travel at the rate of from one to two miles an hour; whereas in Norfolk they step out at not less than three to four miles an hour, and the same, or a greater, agility is preserved in the other departments." In the whole of this book there is no reference by Marshall to any other duties performed by the ploughmen; but he is concerned for the most part with questions of soil and crops, and devotes very little space to hours of work, wages and so forth. I think one is justified in assuming therefore, that here, as in Bedford, the ploughman was expected to prepare his horses for the day's work, and also attend to them at the end of the day, tasks which would probably add another 4 hours to his total! It seems quite certain, that in this particular passage Marshall was concerned only with the actual time spent at the plough, and did not include a period of preparation and a further one of bedding down the horses at the end of the day.

The same argument probably applies to the passage which Rae cites from James and Malcolm's Agriculture of Buckingham (1797; p. 39): "The ploughmen go out at 7 o'clock in the morning in the summer, and return at 3 in the afternoon; in the winter from 8 to 3." But Rae does not mention what follows: "The labourers, in the summer six months, work from 6 to 6, taking half an hour to breakfast and one hour at dinner; and from light to dark in the winter six months, taking the same time at meals as in the summer." It seems likely to me that the ploughman's actual ploughing hours were regulated by the amount that his *horses* could do, but that his actual *working* hours, including other duties, were probably much nearer to those of the labourers!

The final reference, in Marshall's Rural Economy of the West of England (1796), is a brief one, but is open to the same interpretation as the others (I 119): "The hours of work are well-regulated. The plough-teams make two journeys a day as in Norfolk; they go out before 8 in the morning and return at 12, go out again before 2 and return before 6, working about 8 hours a day." I am quite certain that the practices described here were pretty universal, in that stable work was extra; certainly none of the references contradict it. So much for Rae.[91]

Thorold Rogers (p. 394) tells of rules more·in accord with Elizabeth's Act: the magistrates of Warwick regulated the length of working hours on April 9th, 1684 in terms identical with those of 6 Eliz (1562—3), that is a twelve-hour day. In Chamberlayne's Angliae Notitia (ed. 1694 p. 52) it is said: "The natives endure long and hard labour; insomuch that after twelve hours hard work, they will go in the Evening to Foot-ball, Stool-ball, Cricket ..." Just as Markham had done, Sir William Petty, a political economist of the latter half of the 17th century, in his Several Essays in Political Arithmetick (London 1699), found fault with the length of the working day: "Man needs ... labour a twentieth part more, or half an hour per diem extraordinary ... which within common Experience (is) very tolerable." This implies a working day of 10 hours! Miss Elizabeth W. Gilboy, having published Wages in 18th century England (Harvard Univ. Pr. 1934), arrives at the conclusion (p. 8), that "the day was about 11 hours long in 1756, and about 10 hours in 1779 and 1785". This statement is open to doubt; see p. 96 below. However, there may have been some modification of the old arrangements, for in Fielding's Tom Jones (Bk 11 ch. 9) we find: "The sturdy hind now attends the levee of his fellow labourer, the ox; the cunning artificer, the diligent mechanic, spring from their hard mattress; and now the bonny housemaid begins to repair the discorded drum-room (at Bath); while the riotous authors of that disorder, in broken, interrupted slumbers, tumble and toss ... In simple language, the clock

---

[91] The estate-owners themselves were sometimes rather conscientious in their work, and therefore demanded long working hours of their labourers. Cf. a letter from Thomas Gray to Wharton, Sept. 14, 1765: "Lord Strathmore, who is the greatest farmer in this neighbourhood, is from break of day to dark night among his husbandmen and labourers."

had no sooner struck seven, than the ladies were ready for their journey ..." This would imply that work began two hours later than in 1563. But Fielding was no countryman and certainly knew little about the working hours of an estate. Far more reliable is Gay — although not a countryman either, as he explains in A Georgic, inscribed to Mr. Pope — since he spent some time out in the country as the guest of a lord. In Rural Sports (1713) the lines 35 ff. indicate that the farmer and 'th' industrious swain' rise very early for their daily work: "Soon as the morning lark salutes the day, Through dewy fields I take my frequent way, Where I behold the farmer's early care, In the revolving labours of the year." Gay adds (l. 91 ff.) that he also sees when work is over: "... when the ploughman leaves the task of day, And trudging homeward whistles on the way ... No warbling chears the woods; the feather'd choir To court kind slumbers to their sprays retire; When no rude gale disturbs the sleeping trees, Nor aspen leaves confess the gentlest breeze ... Far in the deep the sun his glory hides, A streak of gold the sea and sky divides; The purple clouds their amber linings show ... I behold the fading light, And o'er the distant billows lose my sight." It must be more than 7 p.m. Earlier, Shakespeare had mentioned the larks (Love's Labour's Lost V 2 913): "And merry larks are ploughmen's clocks." In Spring (1728) Thomson also presents us with an early morning picture (l. 26 ff.): "At last from Aries rolls the bounteous sun ... Joyous, the impatient husbandman perceives Relenting nature, and his lusty steers Drives from their stalls to where the well-us'd plough Lies in the furrow, loosen'd from the frost. There unrefusing to the harness'd yoke They lend their shoulder, and begin their toil." Thomson does not, however, tell us when the day's work is over. However, Nicholas Rowe, the poet and dramatist, gives us the approximate time of the day when work is over in Jane Shore V. 1. (1714): (Jane). "Wait then with patience, till the circling hours / Shall bring the time of thy appointed rest, / And lay thee down in death. The hireling thus / With labour drudges out the painful day, / And often looks with long-expecting eyes / To see the shadows rise and be dismissed." Granted that these lines, and similar passages, such as Gray's Elegy in A Country Churchyard ll. 97 ff., are merely a literary convention, the day's work for country swains began when the larks began to warble.

The upper classes had, of course, more leisure. In Shakespeare's A Midsummer Night's Dream (V l. 32) Theseus says: "Come now; what

masques, what dances shall we have To wear away this long age of
three hours Between our after-supper and bedtime? ... Is there no play
To ease the anguish of a torturing hour.[92] Some numbers of The Spectator (317 1712, Addison; 454 1712, Steele) show a complete disregard
of the *beau monde* for any fixed hours of work, an attitude like that
of the brother-rakes of Fielding's Joseph Andrews (Book I ch. viii;
Book III ch. 111).

An unrelieved succession of working days was not tolerated among
the craftsmen and apprentices of the towns, as is shown by the history
of the word *holiday* in the NED. In the 16th century if workmen did
not come to work in the morning, but devoted the day to merry-
making, they made holiday. "Do you knowe that it is holliday, a day
to dance in, and make merry at the Ale house?" (1577). If the workmen
struck a whole day, that was a holiday, but *holiday* also acquired
another sense in "to make holiday", that is, to cease from work, to take
a few hour's freedom. In certain districts of England May Day was
apparently a holiday. In his sixth sermon preached before King
Edward VI on April 12th, 1549, Bishop Latimer told a story from his
own experience: he once had to preach in a parish out in the country,
but when he arrived to the church, there were no church-goers. On
enquiring about it he got the reply: "Sir, this is a busy day with us,
we cannot hear you; it is Robin Hood's day. The parish are gone
abroad to gather for Robin Hood (i. e. to collect money for defraying
the expenses attending the May sports then enacted)." Latimer was
angry and exclaimed: "Robin Hood, a traitor and a thief, to put out a
preacher!" (Parker Soc. publ. 9, 208). Deloney also refers to the Old
English custom at Michaelmas of giving servants leave to change their

---

[92] MARLOWE, Fuscum 39 (Ed. ROBINSON, London. 1826. I—III), describes the life
of a rich loafer: he rises at 10 a.m., at 11 goes to Gill's inn, where he sits till 1 p.m.,
"Then sees a play till six, and sups at seven, And after supper, straight to bed is
gone." — MONTAIGNE, the French essayist, gives an amusing picture of his inborn
laziness in Of Experience: "I am hardly shaken and am slow in all things, be it to
rise, to go to bed, or to my meals. Seven of the clock in the morning is to me an
early hour; and where I may command, I neither dine before eleven nor sup till
after six." — When Gray was in Florence he writes in a letter of July 31, 1740,
(referring, of course, to the hot climate): "Here you shall get up at twelve o'clock,
breakfast till three, dine till five, sleep till six, drink cooling liquors till eight, go to
the bridge till ten, sup till two, and sleep till twelve again." Cf. also Berowne in
Love's Labour's Lost I l. 38 ff.

masters and gather together for merry-making: "It was wont to be an
an old custome in Gloucestershire, that at a certaine time in the yeare,
all such young men and Maidens as were out of service, resorted to a
faire that was kept neere Gloucester there to be readie for any that
would come to hire them, the young men stood all on a row on the one
side, & the Maidens on the other."[93] One day, Shrove Tuesday, was
traditionally allowed to be a workless day for the London apprentices.
Dekker alludes to this in his Shoemaker's Holiday (V 2), where Firk
says: "... Every Shrove Tuesday is our year of jubilee; and when the
pancake-bell rings, we are as free as my lord mayor; we may shut up
our shops, and make holiday. I'll have it called Saint Hugh's Holiday."
In Udall's play Ralph Roister Doister (before 1553) 'there is a scene
(I 3) with Mage Mumblecrust spinning on the distaff, Tibet Talkapace
sewing, and Annot Alyface knitting. They sing songs and try to emulate
each other, until Tibet says: "In good sooth one stoppe more, and I
make holy day."[94] The other meaning of holyday — a day free from
work — is met with in the opening scene of Shakespeare's Julius Caesar.
The tribune Flavius meets in a street a crowd of workmen, and he
exclaims:

> Hence! home, you idle creatures, get you home:
> Is this a holiday? what! know you not,
> Being mechanical, you ought not walk
> Upon a labouring day without the sign
> Of your profession? Speak, what trade art thou?

He is answered by a carpenter and a cobbler; and asks the latter:

> But wherefore art not in thy shop to-day?

and the answer is: "... Indeed, sir, we make holiday, to see Caesar and
to rejoice in his triumph." Firk (in Dekker's Shoemaker's Holiday III 1)

---

[93] DELONEY, Thomas of Reading (ed. Mann), p. 222; COLMAN & GARRICK, The
Clandestine Marriage (1766). III 1 (Sterling, a prosperous merchant, to Sir John
Melvil): "Do you come to market for my daughters, like servants at a statute fair?"
Cf. HALÉVY p. 58, where such gatherings at Michaelmas are said to have occurred
as late as the 19th c.; likewise in Sweden, cf. HJELMQVIST, Förnamn och tillnamn,
(Lund 1903) p. 204.
[94] Compare the habit of German innkeepers of to-day of shouting *Feierabend*
when the closing hour approaches, even when there is no holiday coming on; *Feier-abend* means only "Schluss!", "Verlassen Sie den Lokal!"

7

sees his master and mistress approaching and says: "Mum, here comes my dame and my master. She'll scold, on my life, for loitering this Monday; but all's one, let them all say what they can, Monday's our holiday." This may allude to the early observance of Cobbler's Monday in England.

Comparatively few holidays had a secular sanction — most were holy days, such as Christmas, Easter, and Whitsuntide, on which the craftsmen were free. Before the Reformation the holidays in the Church calendar were regularly observed, but when the Puritans had gained power in the country new laws were enacted prohibiting such holidays as did not coincide with the Sabbath. In February, 1647, the London craftsmen and apprentices petitioned both Houses of Parliament for one free day a month, since they had lost the earlier privilege of visiting their friends and relations, to amuse and refresh themselves on such holidays. The Government then, on July 8th 1647, enacted that all scholars, apprentices and servants should have every second Tuesday as a civic holiday, but (with the clever proviso) only on important and extraordinary occasions. This modification of the traditional holidays did not survive. (Gardiner, History of the Great Civil War, III, London 1891, pp. 152—3.)

The petition mentioned above had the backing of almost all apprentices and craftsmen. It is clear that effective organization had been established among all workers in the same craft and among the crafts themselves. Already in 34 Edw III (1361) all associations between labourers had been forbidden, and Edward VI confirmed this ban in 1548, saying that such trade unions of artificers, handicraftsmen, and labourers had decided how much work they should do in a day, and what hours and times they should work, were contrary to the laws and statutes of the realm. In 1720 the master tailors — i. e. the employers — complained to Parliament that "the Journeymen Tailors in and about the Cities of London and Westminster, to the number of seven thousand and upwards" had lately entered into a combination to raise their wages and leave off working an hour sooner than they used to do.[95]

As has been mentioned above (p. 92) Miss Gilboy estimated that the working hours a day were about 11 in 1756, and about 10 in 1779 and 1785. This would mean a reduction of hours — in the face of

---

[95] Cf. S. & B. Webb, History of Trade Unionism. 1920. p. 31.

growing industrialism. Miss Gilboy's calculations cannot be substantiated; cf. T. S. Ashton, The Industrial Revolution (1949, pp. 122—3) who states that in the 18 c. work lasted from 6 a.m. until it was no longer possible to see.

Another fact bearing upon this question is a provision of 7 George III c. 17 (1768), where it is stated that the working hours of tailors within the city of London and within five miles thereof, were to be from six o'clock in the morning to seven o'clock in the evening, with an interval of only one hour for refreshment. As to miners in Cornwall, Halévy (p. 84) gives us a picture of their working lives: "Perhaps mining was now a harder task than it had been a century earlier. It had become necessary to attack the more difficult seams, to invest more capital in the undertaking, and therefore to require more work from the miners in order to maintain profits. Formerly in Cornwall the miner, on his descent into the mine, had begun by sleeping as long as it takes a candle to burn down. He had then worked for two or three hours, at the conclusion of which he rested for half an hour to smoke a pipe before recommencing work. Half the day had been spent in sleeping and lounging about. (Cf. W. Pryce, Mineralogia Cornubiensis ... 1778, pp. 178—9.) Certainly such a thing was no longer possible in 1815. It is, however, scarcely credible that it had ever been possible, even in the 18th century, outside the tin mines of the south-west. It could never, we may be sure, have been possible in the coal mines of the north." Eric Svedenstjerna, a Swedish engineer, who visited Britain in 1802 and 1803 (Resa, igenom en del af England och Skottland åren 1802 och 1803. Stockholm 1804) notes when visiting Hull (p. 184) that in the ship-yards and docks "both here and in the new dock work began at 7 o'clock in the morning and ended at 6 o'clock in the evening. This is the usual working time in England and it is quite sufficient for a man who, during these hours, wants to use his full strength." He adds (p. 185) that he had the impression that like "our" (the Swedish) Dalecarlians English workmen used not to work too hard (våldarbeta), but went on steadily and did not count the time necessary for such arrangements as would lighten or hasten the work. Svedenstjerna (p. 277) mentions also child labour in a foundry on the Clyde (boys between 10 and 12), but does not give any working hours, only says that sometimes they are better paid than grown-ups in the same work. Gustaf Broling, another Swedish technician, also mentions child labour

(Anteckningar under en resa i England åren 1797, 1798, och 1799. Stockholm 1812. II p. 268) in a coal mine near Norwich: Tom, a boy of 12 or 13 years of age, was entrusted with the mine hoist, which functioned excellently. Another time (II 104) he gives a picture of Leeds on a Sunday afternoon when the pavements were crowded by children. "It always gives a pleasant feeling to see an increasing birth-rate especially since these young citizens of the world are well taken care of in order to make them useful to the state. Already in their sixth or seventh years they begin to assist their parents in simple jobs." He found an instance of this in a house where the father of a family was a 'private' weaver, who had his own little factory run by his children and himself. It seems that they worked even on Sundays.

VI.

The tremendous growth of English industrialism in 1800—1850 demanded more hands, and despite Malthus the progeny of poor families increased. The enclosure policy and other social causes brought many of the rural population to the towns, and they merged with the town labourers. Irishmen used to come across to offer their services at a low price. The mercantilist idea that poor children's work was a blessing to society and themselves contributed also to alleviating the demand for man-power so greedily requested by the factory owners. The workers were denied every weapon to defend themselves: the right of associating to voice a compact demand for more pay and less hours. In this defenceless state of the workers the owners could dictate their own terms: more work and less pay.[96] There is no doubt that working hours increased enormously during the first quarter of the 19th c. The hectic pursuit of wealth of the factory owners at the beginning of that century led to the deliberate subjection of the workers. Fielden of Todmorden, an employer who championed the cause of

---

[96] WADE 241: "The standard of wages has also reference to the hours of labour and periods of relaxation. It has been the policy of masters of late years (ab. 1835) to encroach on operatives in this respect, by cutting off or abridging holidays, and meal-times, and gradually extending the working hours; knowing that an increase of one fourth in the time of labour is equivalent to a reduction in the same proportion in the amount of wages." — MARX (Capital, Nelson's ed.) is full of scorn for Wade (p. 265), but he calculates wages and hours in the same way (p. 247 ff.). See, besides, MARX pp. 48 ff.; 259—264; 265—314; 314—324.

shorter working hours, had inherited a mill, where the working hours were originally 10 a day, but his father had increased them to 12, and on Saturday 11; This was at the end of the 18th century. (Hammond, Town Lab. 30.) Still 12 hours a day had been the normal Elizabethan working day, although it must be admitted that in Queen Elizabeth's day the law applied particularly to husbandmen who worked most of the time in the fields, and to masons, and artisans working in small shops. To work indoors in a large factory for the same number of hours was quite another thing. A pamphlet published in 1823 gives as an example of industrial working hours: "At Tyldesley they work fourteen hours per day, including the nominal hour for dinner; the door is locked in working hours, except half an hour at tea time; the workpeople are not allowed to send for water to drink in the hot factory; and even the rain water is locked up, by the master's order, otherwise they would be happy to drink even that." (Hammond, loc. cit. 20.) At Manchester in 1825 the working hours in mills and mines varied from 12 $\frac{1}{2}$ to 14, and work was carried on day and night. This was generally the case for full-grown men.[97] For women and children the conditions were worse. A report compiled in 1842 (Hammond, loc. cit. 28) cites the case of a married woman who worked 12 hours in the day in the mine, and afterwards at night in the home, washing, cooking, and cleaning her house.[98] Boys employed in mills and mines[99] worked from eighteen to twenty hours a day (Hammond, loc. cit. 28). The explanation of the boys' long hours is found in the suggestion by Locke in 1697 that boys brought up by the parish should be set to work while still at school from the age of three to fourteen (Hammond, loc. cit. 143 ff.); Defoe was delighted to see such youngsters working industriously, as he notes in his Tour thro' the Whole Island (III 145). Many of these boys were apprenticed to employers at the age of seven and upwards, till they were twenty-one. They were completely at the mercy of their masters and a pathetic account of this iniquitous system

---

[97] P. Gaskell, pp. 40 f.; 115 ff.; 138; 217. — Marx p. 48 ff. — Ludlow and Lloyd Jones p. 9. — Hammond, Village Labourer p. 237. — Martin Lamm, August Blanche som Stockholmsskildrare. Uppsala 1931, p. 8: working hours for artisans in Stockholm in the years 1810—1820 were from four in the morning to eight or nine in the evening.

[98] Cf. Thomas p. 273 (1845).

[99] Cf. p. 99 f. above: Jars's statement.

is given in Crabbe's description of the brutality of Peter Grimes.[1] The
parents of these children could do nothing to prevent this, for as late
as 1815 a committee reported that in London relief was "seldom bestowed without the parish claiming the exclusive right of disposing, at
their pleasure, of all the children of the person receiving relief" (Hammond, loc. cit. 145). The length of working-hours increased, as the
mills multiplied and competition between manufacturers at home or
abroad was considered necessary. Boys and even girls were offered by
parents to employers in order to eke out the income of the family on
the same terms as parish children.[2] Generally, therefore, the conditions
under which children were employed were much worse than those of
adult labour.[3] The most pathetic feature of child employment, however, was that children were forced to work in mines and as chimney-
sweeps (Hammond, loc. cit. p. 172 ff.). Small boys and girls were
necessary for sweeping horizontal flues, sometimes only seven inches
broad, or for working in seams and shafts too narrow for older children
or grown-ups. We understand Blake's poems if they are set against the
background of such working conditions. In 1784 night work for children
was forbidden in Manchester, but the restriction was not observed.
Peel's Act of 1802 allowed children to work no more than 12 hours a
day between 6 a.m. and 9 p.m., and night work was forbidden, though
with exceptions![4] In 1816 another bill was passed, despite opposition
in some quarters, that forbade the apprenticeship of parish (and other)
children to masters at a distance above forty miles from their home
parish. Childrens' working conditions had been as severe, or worse,
than those of adults (Hammond, loc. cit. 157): they began work at 5
or 6 a.m. and left off at 7 or 8 p.m., with no time off on Saturdays.
These long hours, 14 or 15 hours daily, were often spent working in a

---

[1] THOMAS p. 7.

[2] THOMAS p. 272.

[3] THOMAS pp. 16, 18 (13 hours a day an ideal working day), 24, 25, 32 (11 1/2
hours are long enough time), 38, 55, 65.

[4] LUDLOW and LLOYD JONES p. 22. — Cf. also ALFRED I 27 f.; In 1796 Dr Per-
cival, a Manchester medical man, exposed the hurtful consequences of the prevailing
working-hours for children and grown-ups. That the Middle Ages looked upon
children in a more "humane" way can be seen in 23 Edw. III, where a male child
under 14 is *non potens in corpore*, while a female child under 12 is *non potens in
corpore*; but 5 Elizabeth makes the situation worse: the age is fixed in both sexes
at 12. (ALFRED I p. 193).

temperature of 75 to 80 degrees F. For meals, they had at the most
half an hour for breakfast and one hour for dinner, but these breaks
were often infringed by forcing children to work while eating.[5] Even
in the face of public indignation employers, or their overseers,[6] made
light of the sufferings of the children. They frankly admitted that the
working-hours of children employed in their factories varied from 6
a.m. to 7 p.m., or, even, from 5 a.m. to 8 p.m., which meant a working
day of from 13 to 15 hours. The Act of 1818 lowered the age at which
children might begin work to 8 years of age, and the maximum working
hours were fixed at 13 a day. The Cotton Factories Regulation Act of
1819 enacted that children between the ages of 9 and 16 might be
employed and their hours of work were fixed at a maximum of 13 $\frac{1}{2}$
which included 1 $\frac{1}{2}$ hours for meals. Children were therefore expected
to work 12 hours a day or 72 hours a week. Night work was forbidden.
(Sir Robert Peel had asked for a reduction to 10 in 1815.) The two
commissioners appointed to see that the act was observed, a magistrate
and a parson, were generally so uninterested that the owners could still
make the children work for 15 or 16 hours a day, with impunity,
making the act wholly ineffectual. In 1825 Hobhouse brought in a bill
intended to prevent these irregularities and to reduce working hours for
children to 11, but the opposition which this proposal aroused made
him suggest finally a Saturday working day of 'only' 9 hours, which
was carried.[7] All this legislation was concerned only with the working

---

[5] Cf. also THOMAS p. 186 f.

[6] Cf. THOMAS pp. 41, 162, 327.

[7] In the Life of George Crabbe (by his son) p. 136, it is said that the poet and
his wife paid a visit in 1787 to Dr Cartwright at Doncaster: "when she entered the
vast building, full of engines thundering with resistless power, yet under the apparent
management of children, the sight of the little creatures condemned to such a mode
of life in their days of natural innocence, quite overcame her feelings, and she burst
into tears". — Another indictment of juvenile labour comes from Southey in Espriella's
Letters from England (1807; Letter XXXVIII), one of the earliest detailed descrip-
tions of a textile factory and the employer's callous indifference to his young
workers. "The poor must be kept miserably poor, or such a state of things could
not continue ... They would not be crowded in hot taskhouses by day, and herded
together in damp cellars at night; they would not toil in unwholesome employments
from sun-rise to sun-set, whole days, and whole days and quarters, for with twelve
hours labour the avidity of trade is not satisfied ...". See also SOUTHEY, Essays,
Moral and Political I 75—155; Colloquies I 148—99. — HALÉVY p. 86. — Life of
Owen pp. 155 f.; 157 ff.; 160 ff. OWEN, Address at New Lanark p. 110 (concerning

hours of children. In March, 1834, a Factory Act limited the work of children under 11 years of age to eight hours a day. This gave an impetus to lessen the working hours even of youths and grown-ups and to demand an eight hours' day being the maximum of time for them to labour (the Webbs p. 132). As a matter of fact, already in 1819 when the Act about the health of young persons in cotton factories had been passed, the Quarterly Review, wholly on the side of the 'young persons', wrote, "The truth, however, is that it is a bill to limit the hours of labour of *all persons* employed in cotton factories, whatever may be their age. Every person acquainted with cotton spinning knows, that so soon as the younger persons employed cease working, the more advanced must cease likewise; the labour is so connected, that they must cease or go on together." (Thomas p. 26.)

the formation of character); idem, The Manufacturing System p. 124: Owen suggests that children ought not to be employed in mills to look after machinery until they were ten years old, or that they should not be employed more than six hours per day until they were twelve years old. Idem ibid. 126 f.: Owen demolishes the arguments of the employers, that a reduction of working hours from 14 or 15 to 12 hours a day would mean higher prices, by suggesting that the consumers will have to bear the increased prices. Even so he does not believe that prices would rise. At any rate national health would be better, and so, in the end, the employers would gain. — Idem, On the Employment of Children in Manufactories (a letter to the Earl of Liverpool): pp. 131, 133, 134. — Idem, To the British Master Manufacturers, p. 142: No child should work indoors until 12 years of age except, if necessary, in certain trades, and then the child must work no more than six hours a day between the ages of ten and twelve years of age. Ten hours daily work were not even required from Negro slaves. — P. GASKELL p. 136; 141: "The hours of labour have not undergone any very material alteration since the universal application of steam, and since the doing away with night labour as a general custom"; 159: (evidence before a committee) "Had five hundred children from five to eight years of age; work thirteen hours, one hour and a half for meals". — WADE 113: 1 & 2 Wm IV c. 39, (1831): ... "in no cotton mill, where steam or water power is used to work machinery, shall any person under twenty-one years of age be allowed to work at night; that is between the hours of half-past eight in the evening and half-past five in the morning; and that no person under eighteen years of age shall work more ... than twelve hours in one day, nor more than nine hours on a Saturday; and that every such person be allowed, in the course of one day, one hour and half for meals." Cf. also THOMAS p. 25: Provisions for the Regulation of Cotton Mills and Factories, July 2, 1819; and ib. 26 Ashley's argument; p. 153 (1839). — MARX 263. — LUDLOW and LLOYD JONES p. 10. — HAMMOND, Town Labourer pp. 168—70. — ALFRED I 37, 45, 52, 55, 96, 164, 175, 282—306; II 70, 72, 83, 86, 87, 188—208, 229, 271; DRIVER 238.

It is not necessary to enter into detail about the increased number of working hours of all the categories of work-people. There are so many books written on English industrialism that a sorting out of the number of hours must seem superfluous. Mr. and Mrs. Hammond have in their books brought together material enough to convince everybody. In 1948 Dr. Maurice Walton Thomas published The Early Factory Legislation, a most impartial and objective survey; the factory inspectors began their work by believing factory owners and magistrates, but soon they had their eyes opened to the social ills and the evasions of the 'millocrats', and Dr. Thomas bases his work principally on their reports. Reports of Government committees; cross-examinations of industrial witnesses; and historians of the day and later; all concur in giving data about the increase in the number of working hours. With the increased number of hours, even for small children, followed human misery. The social aspects of early British industrialism will be found in the Hammonds. Its strictly economic aspects are given, among others, by Prof. T. S. Ashton, whose work The Industrial Revolution (1949), however, also gives sidelight on human suffering of the epoch; he quotes with approval the Hammonds' statement that "Young lives were spent at best in monotonous toil, at worst in a hell of human cruelty" (p. 113). "Obviously abominations of this kind cannot be excused by pointing to the advantages of industrialisation — advantages which could have been secured as well or better if measures had been taken to prevent the scandals in question", Prof. Tawney writes in a letter to the author (April 19, 1953), and continues, "If Ashton does not in his book dwell at length on the social evils of the industrial revolution the reason is not that he is unaware of or indifferent to them, or that he disputes their evidence. It is merely that that subject has already been dealt with at great length in other works, for example those of the Hammonds, whom he admires, and that he is concerned in his own to explain the economic aspects of the movement, to which less attention has been devoted." Still Ashton seems to object to a historian's view: "the disasters of the industrial revolution" (p. 161), and says, "The central problem of the age was how to feed and clothe and employ generations of children outnumbering by far those of any earlier time ... (England) was delivered, not by her rulers, but by those who, seeking no doubt their own narrow ends, had the wit and resource to devise new instruments of production and new methods of adminis-

tering industry . . ., from Asiatic standards." But if such a strictly
economic view of the process is taken, how can we then reproach
Soviet Russia to-day for her labour camps, forced labour by political
prisoners, etc.? Everything must be quite in order because they serve the
end: the industrialization of the country. It would, of course, be foolish
to reproach the age as a whole for tolerating these conditions since the
moral standards of one age are not those of another. Ideals change as
time passes, and it is quite probable that mind and conscience travel
more slowly than technical progress. To understand the attitude of early
nineteenth century England we must look back into the 18th century
of the whole of Europe. The callous attitude of that century to the
labouring class is easily distinguished; it is clear how, on this basis, the
blind egotism of the men of the new industrial age came into being.
English industrialism begun in the 1770's made the rift between employers and employed even deeper. The development of machine power,
the expansion of markets, and the consolidation of capital, organized in
mighty undertakings, led to a degradation of the human factor: man-
power. Despite the illusion of personal freedom the labourers and workmen lived in effectual slavery, without enjoying the interest shown by
the slave owner for his personal property: the slaves. While the workers
were thus deprived of every vestige of personal liberty and dignity by
the demands of their masters, their appeals to authority and law were
unregarded. What little of their rights remained to them was wrung
from them by conscious anti-labour legislation. When through the irony
of History some precedent tended to support the claims of the workers,
it was hastily annulled. As soon as trade experienced a surprise boom
and left the workers with the chance of bettering their condition, which
previous laws had not foreseen, the masters appealed to Parliament,
and Parliament issued fresh laws with a distinct anti-labour bias. If
Byron and Shelley are read against this social background, criticism of
their so-called fanaticism must fall flat; their verse is seen as the
expression of well-justified indignation.

Adam Smith's new ideas on political economy were revolutionary;
they exploded the theory that there should necessarily be cut-throat
competition between countries for trade and that a prosperous country
could only exist among poor neighbours. Smith, however, did not
approve of the current ideas that workers were incapable of taking care
of themselves and their income, if it was more than mere subsistence.

Instead he had spoken for higher wages and a modification of working hours. But this side of his gospel was quite forgotten by the employers. When they heard about 'the obvious and simple system of natural liberty', they took this to mean that every law for the control of monopolies, which would otherwise exploit the public, and for the regulation of wages should be done away.[8] The next step was to idealize the employer for being an enlightened egotist. Since it was the aim of every employer to make as much profit as possible, he had to see to it that his workmen were fit; thus he had to give them reasonable wages so that they could yield the best result, — if not, he would suffer himself. Hence, an employer would be foolish if he were to hurt his workmen! But this is the philosophy of the slave owner: he has bought his slaves and they represent an outlay of capital. If they are molested, starved, or otherwise hurt, he suffers a loss. But in a country where the prerequisite of a slave society, the cash purchase of slaves, does not exist, but where instead every worker is a 'free' man, an employer is not responsible for his workmen outside the factories. The theory did not hold water when applied to conditions in England. Burke wrote: "It is therefore the first and fundamental interest of the labourer that the farmer should have a full incoming profit on the product of his labour. The proposition is self-evident, and nothing but the malignity, perverseness ... and particularly the envy they bear to each other's prosperity, could prevent their seeing and acknowledging it, with thankfulness to the benign and wise Disposer of all things, who obliges men, whether they will or not, in pursuing their own selfish interests, to connect the general good with their own individual success!" The last thought is borrowed straight from Shaftesbury, but basically, Burke's argument is that of the slave owner. Burke then asks: "But if the farmer is excessively avaricious? Why, so much the better — the more he desires to increase his gains, the more interested is he in the good condition of those upon whose labour his gains must principally depend!" Is it possible that Burke seriously believed this?[9]

---

[8] Cf. ASHTON p. 139; THOMAS p. 202: Lord Ashley said in Parliament on Feb. 12, 1844, "That the State had a right to watch over the moral and physical well-being of the people was recognized by all civilised governments, and nowhere was the problem more acute than in this country, where the numbers engaged in the textile industry approached half a million."

[9] BURDETT: "no one gave less to labour than it was the interest of the labourer to receive". (HAMMOND, Town Lab. 200.) Such an opinion could lead to resistance

With the acceptance of this view of the relations between employers
and employed every reform, even for bettering the conditions of child
labour, was resisted by the employers. Another doctrine, which had
pernicious consequences, was that payment for work was regulated by
natural laws.[10] The well-being of the workman was at the mercy of
natural forces. Here we see the influence of Pope's (and Leibniz's)

---

against any reform, for instance the reduction of working hours for children. — For
criticism of the various systems which up to then had governed the world by
privileged classes, masters, etc., see OWEN, A New View of Society 86; idem, On
the Employment of Children 138; idem, An Address of the Working Class 152.

Burdett's use of the word *labour* is interesting: it must mean "the labouring class",
for note the preposition *to*, not *for*, as it ought to have been if *labour* had meant
work. In MURRAY's A New English Dictionary the term *labour* as meaning a body
of workmen (as distict from a body of capitalists) is given not earlier than 1880.
But how are we then to interpret *labour* in the following quotation from H. J. PYE's
Alfred (p. 59; 1801),

> Here in full colours to my eyes are shown,
> The true supporters of the regal throne;
> 'Tis from industrial Labour's hard-earn'd bread,
> That Opulence is decked and Luxury fed ...

where Opulence, Luxury, and, later, Commerce, stand for social groups and activities? On the same page there are lines such as "The bark itself was rear'd on Labour's
field ... from rustic Labour springs the iron frame ... While Labour's hardy son
the blast defies." Surely Pye's Labour does not mean *work*, but 'labouring people',
'labourers', that is, a collective term for that class of society. Other passages in
various authors of the period support this interpretation: DISRAELI, The Revolutionary
Epick (1836) p. 69: "Patient Labour Restless becomes and sickens of the toil"; ib.
p. 118: "The sacred rights of Labour"; idem, Sybil (1845), Bk III ch. iv. p. 187,
speaking of an area (Woodgate) with few great employers: "Here Labour reigns
supreme"; ibid. Bk V ch. i (p. 337): "the rights of Labour were as sacred as those
of property", i. e. the rich; ibid. Bk V ch. x (p. 391): "the principal champions of
the cause of Labour" (i. e. the labouring class). Cf. also in the same book, Bk V
ch. i (p. 336): "Wealth and Work"; Bk VI ch. v (p. 425): "When Toil plays,
Wealth ceases. — When Toil ceases, the People suffer, said Sybil.", that is, when
the workmen strike, the masters suffer; when the workmen are unemployed the
people suffer. Further, idem, Coningsby Bk 7 ch. 2: "labour is his twin brother".
The origin of this use of *Labour* must be that already in the 18th c. it was a convenient collective name for the labouring classes among the employers. Cf. [AKEN-
SIDE &] DYER (1757), The Poet. Works (1855) p. 105: "... No land With more
variety of wealth rewards the hand of Labour"; ib. p. 107: "... may the hand
Of mighty Labour drain their gusty lakes".

[10] "The Committee believe that the hours of labour are limited by natural laws,
which cannot be violated with impunity." Report of Committee on the Baking Trade
in Ireland, in KARL MARX, Capital 281.

theories. The economic teaching that workmen should be kept on a level of mere subsistence did its insiduous work. In France Turgot had expressed this idea in his phrase: "Il (the workman) ne gagne que sa vie!" If the workman wished to save, he had to change his diet for the worse. Malthus also helped indirectly to strengthen the views of the capitalist. He had said that the population increases more rapidly than the means to support it, or, than the chances of existence. The cake could not expand as quickly as the number of eaters. Hence, poverty was unavoidable. In the 18th century it had been said that poor people were the blessing of a state (because they could be forced to work — at low prices); now it was thought that births ought to be restricted, otherwise vice and misery would increase, as consequences of poverty. How was this theory accepted by the ruling class? They agreed that poverty could not be avoided. Hence every reform tending to alleviate poverty was a dangerous interference with natural order. For if the poor thought that there might be attempts to better their position they would become optimistic and increase the population.

Ever since the Black Death the authorities had been anxious to prevent any association of labourers (and, later, of factory hands) in order to obtain higher wages. By 1800 about forty different measures forbidding such 'conspiracy' were on the statute book. The punishment for such breaches of the law were heavy, but a workman was nominally allowed to appeal — if he deposited £ 20! In spite of opposition in both houses of Parliament, the Act of 1800 forbade the association of working men. It is worth recording that Wilberforce, who championed the emancipation of Negro slaves, not only supported a petition from a group of employers to prevent trade unions in their branch of industry, but suggested that the legislation against working men should be extended to all trades and industries. Unless there was a generally applicable combination law the 'disease' of combining would harm society. Wilberforce and Pitt carried the day. No combination of workmen was allowed, and they were wholly at the mercy of their employers. In 1824 a new Combination Law was enacted (5 Geo IV c. 96) which repealed all laws, previously made, against workmen who combined together to advance or fix the rate of wages or to alter the hours of working. In the following year this act was amended, and left workmen individually and collectively free in the disposal of their labour. But prosecution for conspiracy was maintained.

Negro Slavery was for half a century or more a sore for English liberal opinion; Wilberforce was *the* champion for its abolition. The literary efforts to rouse the country against this evil came from many sources; suffice it here to mention Cowper, Wordsworth, Southey, Campbell, Hannah More.[10a] A large number of poems were written on moral principles against the traffic in human flesh, "black ivory". Miss More's Poems (1816; many dating from the 18 c.) discuss "The Black Slave Trade" (p. 371), in which the usual invocation of Liberty and other *clichés* occur, and there is the following righteous outburst (p. 379):

> And Tempe's vale, and parch'd Angola's sand,
> One equal fondness of their sons command.
> Th'unconquer'd Savage laughs at pain and toil
> Basking in Freedom's beams which gild his native soil.
> Does thirst of empire, does desire of fame,
> (For these are specious crimes,) our rage inflame?
> No: sordid lust of gold their fate controls,
> The basest appetite of basest souls;
> Gold, better gain'd by what their ripening sky,
> Their fertile fields, their arts, and mines supply.
> What wrongs, what injuries does Oppression plead,
> To smooth the crime and sanctify the deed?

or we read (p. 382): "Spartans and Helots see with different eyes: / *Their* miseries philosophic quirks deride, / Slaves groan in pangs disown'd by Stoic pride." She does not mince her words, but calls the capitalist (p. 384) "thou, White Savage". All this could, with as much legitimate indignation, have been addressed to the factory owners in Britain who exploited children and grown-up workers in the same way.[10b] But Miss More did not find such a theme worthy of her pen. Once, however, she wrote an essay, The White Slave Trade (ib. 391): "Hints towards framing a Bill for the Abolition of the White Female Slave Trade, in the Cities of London and Westminster", but it proves to be a

---

[10a] See further WYLIE SYPHER's sarcastic book Guinea's Captive Kings: British Anti-Slavery Literature of the XVIIIth Century. Univ. of North Carolina Press. Chapel Hill 1942.

[10b] Cf. SYPHER, loc. cit. p. 212: Boswell's picture of social conditions in England in comparison with Negro Slavery.

facetious lampoon against young society ladies being obliged to dress sumptuously and to attend teas and dinners! The ladies should be freed from the tyranny of Fashion, that is all.

This ignorance of the social facts in England, or this attitude of non-committal, obtained practically everywhere. It was Richard Oastler — see Cecil Driver, Tory Radical (Oxford Univ. Press) 1946, and Alfred, The History of the Factory Movement, I, II, 1857 — who introduced the term (*white*) *slavery* for factory workers in England and thus was led to compare the lot of Negro slaves in America with that of child and grown-up workers in Britain. Oastler's first letter on the factory question in 1830 (Alfred I 98) had the headline "Yorkshire Slavery", since then repeatedly used by him in newspaper articles, pamphlets, etc.[11] In that very first letter he quotes a poem,

> Vow one by one, vow altogether, vow
> With heart and voice, eternal enmity
> Against oppression by our brethren's hands;
> Till man nor woman under Britain's laws,
> Nor son, nor daughter, born within her empire,
> Shall buy, or sell, or Hire, or Be a Slave.

He continues, "The nation is now most resolutely determined that negroes shall be free. Let them, however, not forget that Britons have common rights with Afric's sons." (Alfred I 101.) His second letter, Oct. 20th, 1831, (Alfred I 118), also compares the two slaveries: "... no man ... can really wish to emancipate the poor black slave in the West Indies, who refuses you his aid and assistance in emancipating *your* children from a slavery more horrid than that by which the infants of the slaves in the West Indies are cursed. ... never forget that these 'liberal factory masters' are not quite so 'liberal' as the tyrannical slaveholder! The latter provides for his slaves when they are weak, or maimed, or sick, or aged, and when they can no longer work. But the former, with a 'liberality' unknown in the West Indies, after they have maimed or weakened their work-people, or when they have worked them till they can work no more, turn them out, *for you who can work to support*, thus swelling the poor rates and lessening your earnings."

---

[11] Oastler, Yorkshire Slavery (1835); Slavery in Yorkshire (1835?); Damnation! (1837).

How difficult it was for even a highly educated and intellectual man to grasp this simple statement of fact is seen in a letter from Macaulay in 1832 (Alfred I 148): "Permit me to add one word on the subject of the Order in Council, which has been sent to St. Lucie. That Order, as you justly say, has provided that a slave shall be forced to work only nine hours a day, and only five days a week. But you forget, I think, that the slave has to find his own subsistence besides. The time which is secured to him is not holiday time. He must cultivate his own provision-ground during the hours when he is absent from his master's sugar plantation ... There is, therefore, not the slightest analogy between the case of a freeman of mature years. The law ought to limit the hours of forced labour of the slave: — and why? Because he is a slave. Because he has no power to help himself. But the freeman cannot be forced to work to the ruin of his health. If he works over hours, it is because it is his own choice to do so. The law ought not to protect him; for he can protect himself."[12] Macaulay, a Whig, shared the same view as Bentham, another Whig (Thomas p. 48 footn. 7).

In Huddersfield in 1836 (Alfred II 92) the remonstrants included the following paragraph in their petition: "Your remonstrants, however, can never forget that 20.000.000 *l.* have been paid, out of the labour of these children, to purchase for the black adults eight hours' labour per day, and that the friends of the negro are in motion, with a view of obtaining more power, and a new act to enforce the eight hours' act in Jamaica." But "the little white factory slaves" should go on working to the utmost of their strength, and even further: here the humanity of the government ended. Lord Ashley, in the 2nd reading, 1836, most aptly called attention to the discrepancy of the treatment of

---

[12] On the other hand, cf. COLERIDGE (Inquiring Spirit, ed. COBURN, 1951), who wrote in 1818 (p. 351 et seq.) "Remarks ... on Sir Robert Peel's Bill": "But *free* Labour! — in what sense, not utterly sophistical, can the labour of children, extorted from the want of their parents, 'their poverty, but not their will, consenting', be called *free*?" And again: "It is our duty to declare aloud, that if the labour were indead free, the employer would purchase and the labourer sell, what the former has no right to buy, and the latter no right to dispose of: namely, the labourer's health, life and well-being." The last phrase is typically Coleridgian. — SOUTHEY writes in Espriella, Letters from England (1807; Letter XXVI): "We talk of the liberty of the English, and they talk of their own liberty: but there is no liberty in England for the poor." Cf. also my paper, Charles Dickens' sociala kritik, in the literary review Edda (Oslo 1952).

West Indian slaves and that of English workers (Thomas p. 92): "Let hon. members recollect that the Negro Emancipation Act contained a clause providing that the negro population of the British colonies should not work more than forty-five hours per week. Would the House increase this time if the planters said this was not sufficient to remunerate them?"

Since this reference to a working-day of eight hours put in action in Jamaica is of special interest, I have had it examined through the courtesy of the Colonial Office library. As a matter of fact it has not been possible to trace any provision in the Jamaican legislation for an *exact* eight hour day. It is then the more remarkable that the Huddersfield remonstrants considered the working-hours in Jamaica to be an eight hours' day, — Ashley had spoken of 45 hours a week, thus less than 8 hours a day. This shows that a notion of an eight hours' day was in the air and found practicable. The reason why it did not obtain, or became the avowed slogan of the labour movement in those days, will be given below.

On the 12th December 1833 following upon the passing of the United Kingdom Act for the abolition of slavery in the British Colonies (3 & 4 Will 4 Chapter 73) the Government of Jamaica enacted a law for the same purpose (4 Will 4 Chapter 41 in the Jamaica series).

Part of section 47 of the Jamaica Act reads as follows: — "And whereas one day in every fortnight has heretofore been allowed to the slaves for the cultivation of their provision-grounds, so as to make the number of days twenty-six in the year for the purpose aforesaid, exclusive of Sundays and holidays: And whereas, a provision made in this act confines the hours of labour which the master is entitled to from such praedial labourer to forty-five hours, or five days of nine hours each in any one week: And whereas a further allowance for the cultivation of their grounds and the raising and securing the crops grown thereon, is allotted to them by the act of the imperial parliament hereinbefore recited: Be it enacted, That from and after the first day of August next, every praedial apprenticed labourer shall be entitled to four hours and one half of an hour, out of the five and forty weekly working hours hereinbefore mentioned, for the cultivation of his or her grounds, and such portion of time shall be allowed to each apprentice, either on any day or days in any one week, or by any number of days consecutively, at such period of the year as may be deemed by the

8

possessor or manager of such property least detrimental and injurious
to the cultivation of the plantation on which he or she shall reside, and
the gathering in of the crop and the manufacture of the produce thereof; and any person entitled to the service of any such praedial apprenticed labourer, who shall refuse to allow such portion of time to any
such labourer, shall be subject and liable to a penalty of forty shillings
for each offence, to be recovered as hereinafter provided . . ."

It will be seen from the above extract that the net working hours
per week of a praedial labourer totalled 40 ¹/₂, which, spread over five
days, amounted to a fraction over 8 hours per day. Neither the preamble nor the rest of the Act throws any further light on the matter.
It must be borne in mind, however, that this legislation was due to
working conditions described above before the abolition of slavery.
Still, the mere fact that more humane working hours had been introduced among the former slaves, led the English workmen to believe
that the 8 hours' day had been realized in the West Indies.

It is a melancholy fact that the introduction of machines to increase
the output made industrialists think of human beings as machines. The
machines were expensive and should yield a good interest in as short
time as possible. They should not be idle even in the night hours. When
machines were being applied to industry unemployment was at first the
inevitable consequence. Ashton (p. 133) has also mentioned the riots of
the textile villages. But the employers were stronger, and the workers
had to flock to the factories to get work in order to live. Then the
employers demanded more work, i. e. time, from the workmen: they
should keep time with the machines. In societies where machines had
not been introduced the old patriarchal system continued: the employers
knew from experience that to work efficiently man needed food and
repose, just as domestic animals.[13] Thus, in such societies the demand
for more hours did not arise, — the already existing working time was,
besides, quite considerable as it was; the agricultural labourers and the
slaves in the West Indies went on working according to the statutes.
But the industrial societies had mostly machines which were able to
work twentyfour hours a day if man-power was at hand. Therefore
man was supposed to be able to work as hard as machines. Southey
relates in Espriella's Letters from England (Letter III; 1807): "The life

---

[13] THOMAS p. 290.

of a post-horse is truly wretched: — there will be cruel individuals in all countries, but cruelty here is a matter of calculation: the post-masters find it more profitable to overwork their beasts and kill them by hard labour in two or three years, than to let them do half the work and live out their natural length of life. In commerce, even more than in war, both men and beasts are considered merely as machines, and sacrificed with even less compunction." To judge from the lively and bustling traffic on the roads in Southey's letter the coaches drawn by horses were the motor-cars and buses of the day, i. e. machines.

It is evident that British workmen and labourers were unable to carry on propaganda for shorter working hours. What interested them above all was higher wages, living wages. In some way they may have been afraid of shorter hours, for that might have involved a reduction of their existing wages. Besides, as has been shown above, they had no organizations for carrying through such a campaign.[14] There is no doubt that workmen often believed that working hours had once been shorter and that there was some particular justification for an eight hour day. These were day-dreams, however, rather than certain knowledge. The hours of work had never been eight a day.

In 1891 Sidney Webb (later Lord Passfield) and Harold Cox published their book: The Eight Hours Day. The authors write there (p. 13): "We have been unable to trace the origin of the feeling that Eight Hours constitutes, in some mysterious way, the "natural" or fitting length of the working day. It is well known that the "three eights" have been one of the leading aspirations of the English artisan for, at any rate, fifty years. (See George Howell, The Conflicts of Labour and Capital 1878, chap. VI, sec. 30.) The common tradition, which assigns the origin of the idea to Alfred's division of his time into eight hours work, eight hours sleep, and eight hours recreation and study, is somewhat fanciful. Much more probable is the theory that the equal threefold division of the 24 hours, has, of itself, commended the idea of the eight hours as *specially* reasonable. The following common rhyme, in which the idea is embodied —

> "Eight hours to work, eight hours to play,
> Eight hours to sleep, eight 'bob' a day",

---

[14] OWEN, To The British Master Manufacturers 143: workmen are not free individuals and cannot influence the fixing of working hours; Report to Lanark 251: the working classes made the slaves of an artificial system of wages; COLE, Attempts.

is perhaps of Australian origin,[15] as it does seem that no aspiration for wages of eight shillings a day has yet so much as entered the heads of any considerable section of English workmen. Mr. George Howell suggests that this fourth eight may have been added merely to complete the rhyme.

"A more convincing origin of the ideal of an Eight Hours Day is found in the practice of the fifteenth century. The late Professor J. E. Thorold Rogers states emphatically of that golden age that "it is plain that the day was one of eight hours" (idem, Work and Wages, abridg. ed. 28). But it appears that overtime was worked. At p. 175 of his useful little volume, we find the following [and then follows a quotation in which Rogers tries to make it probable that spread over the whole year work was eight hours a day, nay, even a 48 hours week prevailed. See above 84 ff. G. L.]: "The artisan who is demanding at this time an eight hours day in the building trades, is simply striving to recover what his ancestor worked by four or five centuries ago.

"Those who have any experience of the length of time that traditions linger among an illiterate class will not think it altogether fanciful to suppose that the modern ideal of an Eight Hours Day is the half-forgotten survival from a long-cherished memory of a former shorter day."

Messrs. Webb and Cox also add (p. 13): "there is no magic in the number eight". — The reference to the longevity of oral traditions is apt, but this applies generally to periods when the art of writing is restricted to a few, and the art of printing is unknown. In his History of Irish Literature Stephen Gwynn uses the same argument: the Irish peasants had early lost their soil to the Norman feudal barons, but their songs and tales taught them that originally they had been the rightful owners of the land, and these songs and tales might be considered as title-deeds. I do not deny that traditions survive. But a tradition invented in the late 19th century could not possibly exist in the 16th, 17th, and 18th centuries.[16] It is, indeed, surprising that Sidney Webb

---

[15] This is denied by W. E. Murphy, History of the Eight Hour Movement. Melbourne 1896, p. 5, but none the less true.

[16] Owen, The Effect of the Manufacturing System 122 f.: "Not more than thirty years since, the poorest parents thought the age of fourteen sufficiently early for their children to commence regular labour ... It should be remembered also that twelve hours per day, including the time for regular rest and meals, were then

arrived at such a faulty conclusion. The validity of Professor Thorold Rogers's thesis is undermined by the facts given (pp. 49 f., 84 ff.) above, as well as by Steffen and Cunningham. Rogers's interpretation of the working hours laid down in the Acts of 1495 and 1562—63, as meaning 9 $^1/_2$ hours of work a day can be disproved. There can be no "tradition" about a thing that never existed. We can, however, appreciate the factors which produced this pseudo-tradition by taking into consideration the increased working hours in the early years of the 19th century. Webb and Cox are, on the other hand, too dogmatic in rejecting the suggestion that King Alfred's threefold division of the day had a bearing on the formation of the 19th c. idea of an Eight Hours Day. Sidney and Beatrice Webb, (English Social Government: English Poor Law History. Part I. The Old Poor Law. London 1927) record (p. 2) another threefold division though not of day and night. "Whether or not, as it is alleged, Pope Gregory charged St. Augustine to insist in England on a tripartite division of the tithe, this is what we find in the ordinance ascribed in the eighth century to Egbert, Archbishop of York. 'The priests', he ordained, 'are to take tithes of the people, and to make a written list of the names of the givers, and according to the authority of the canons they are to divide them in the presence of men that fear God. The first part they are to take for the adornment of the church; but the second they are in all humility, mercifully to distribute with their own hands for the use of the poor and strangers; the third part, however, the priests may reserve for themselves.' Exactly such a division was confirmed, in the eleventh century, by a law of Ethelred. 'The King and the Witan have chosen and said, as right it is,

---

thought sufficient to extract all the working strength of the most robust adult; when it may be remarked local holidays were much more frequent than at present in most parts of the kingdom ..." But at the time of writing: "In the manufacturing districts it is common for parents to send their children of both sexes at seven or eight years of age, in winter as well as summer, at six o'clock in the morning, sometimes of course in the dark, and occasionally amidst frost and snow, to enter the manufactories ... and very frequently continue until twelve o'clock at noon, when an hour is allowed for dinner, after which they return to remain, in a majority of cases, till eight o'clock at night." — The "30 years ago" refer back to 1790, when more humane conditions may have existed. But when MARX, Capital 282, says that railwaymen in 1866 declared that about 1854 they had had only eight hours work a day, one must disbelieve them. At that time eight hours of work was unheard of. But the use of that particular figure is interesting.

that one-third part of the tithe which belongs to the Church, shall go
to the reparation of the Church; and a second part to the servants of
God, and a third to God's poor and needy men in thraldom.'" But this
brings us back to Old English history, for this tripartite division was
also practised by King Alfred. Besides, the threefold division of the
tithe was universally applied in all Christendom, not only in England.
It seems safe not to derive William of Malmesbury's division of day
and night from this Catholic economic prescription.

From the very start Robinson Crusoe divided his day into hours for
work, hunting, leisure, and sleep. Crusoe writes in his Journal, Nov. 4
(Tauchnitz edn. p. 59): "This morning I 'began to order my times of
work, of going out with my gun, time of sleep, and time of diversion
(which, by the way, is a threefold division. G. L.); viz. every morning
I walked out with my gun for two or three hours, if it did not rain;
then employed myself to work till about eleven o'clock; then eat what
I had to live on; and from twelve to two lay down to sleep, the
weather being excessively hot; and then, in the evening to work again.
The working part of this day and of the next were wholly employed in
making my table ..." We do not get any fixed number of hours for
each task and for sleep. But one might infer that Defoe had the story
about Alfred in his mind. Incidentally it should be remembered that in
Colonel Jack Defoe says that Jack had Speed's English History in his
library. Defoe consequently knew of the Alfredian tradition. I have
shown above that the Alfredian tradition was a recurrent theme in
literature during practically every decade of the 17th and 18th centuries. The threefold division was not mentioned in Thomson's play,
Alfred, but through Thomson's portrait, Alfred came to be regarded as
a champion of liberty, a noble and pious monarch, a very model of a
man. Thomson also pays homage to him in Summer l. 1479, and in
Liberty IV l. 733. Cowper refers to Alfred in Table Talk (I p. 4).
Robert Burns wrote a poem in memory of Thomson and apostrophized
Alfred in Libertie, A Vision l. 61. Wordsworth mentions Alfred (together with Canute) in A Fact and An Imagination (1816): "her darling
Alfred"; and, further, in Ecclesiastical Sonnets (1820) XXVI, and
XXVII. In sonnet XXVI are the lines: "Ease from this noble miser of
his time No moment steals", which was not explained by Wordsworth
in his own notes. This shows that he took it for granted that everybody
of his own time knew that Alfred had invented a means of measuring

time, if not also his threefold division of the day. In The Warning (1833) Wordsworth writes of "the Crown Of Saxon liberty that Alfred wore". Likewise Shelley refers to Alfred in Ode to Liberty (ix, ll. 121 ff.): "A thousand years the Earth cried, 'Where art thou (Liberty)?' And then the shadow of thy coming fell On Saxon Alfred's olive-cinctured brow." Keats couples together the names of Alfred and Kosciusko, and of Alfred and William Tell (To Kosciusko; Sleep and Poetry ll. 385 f.; Epistle to G. F. Mathew ll. 65 ff.; and to Ch. C. Clarke l. 70, respectively). Coleridge (Table Talk) speaks of Alfred's just laws; Southey refers to Alfred in Colloquies (I 104 f.); and in Little Dorrit (II, ch. 22) Dickens mentions "Saxon Alfred" of all the old kings in England. At his accession to the throne William IV was called "our second Alfred" by the Spectator. (See Early Victorian England, ed. by G. M. Young, II 46.) In Coningsby (1844; Bk 4, ch. 13) Disraeli makes Sidonia say: "Sects rise and sects disappear. Where are the Fifth-Monarchymen? England is governed by Downing Street; once it was governed by Alfred and Elizabeth." [17] The most interesting of all references is the following.

In 1857 Samuel Kydd, an intimate friend of Oastler's, published his important work The History of the Factory Movement, but instead of his own name he put simply Alfred on the title-page. In Cecil Driver's biography of Richard Oastler: Tory Radical there is a reference to Kydd's work (p. 518), and Prof. Driver adds: "The author uses the pseudonym 'Alfred' for reasons that have never become apparent." In the light of what has here been brought together about Alfred's popularity we cannot escape the thought that Kydd wanted to impress his readers by choosing this symbol of social justice and statesmanship. On the other hand, he could not mention his name, since that would have involved a reference to his threefold division of the day and, consequently, 8 hours' work. For Kydd was a sworn adherent of the ten hours' day, which had been so vehemently advocated by his true friend Richard Oastler.

It is true that none of the previous references touched upon the threefold division of the day. All these poetic references to Alfred as

---

[17] Sir Philip Sidney's ideal of a perfect monarch, Euarchus in Arcadia (see ZAND-VOORT, Sidney's Arcadia, Amsterdam 1929, pp. 150—154) may, or may not, be derived from Alfred.

the noble fighter for freedom must have been implemented by the Alfredian tradition of the King's division of the day, in chronicles and histories. As to Walter Scott he was a Scotsman. He did not interest himself in Old English history; the Ivanhoe episode occurs after 1066. It is remarkable, however, that Scott never refers to the Alfredian tradition in his Journal (ed. J. G. Tait, 1950), where he repeatedly speaks of his division of the day. But there are half-veiled allusions to the tradition in two novels; in Rob Roy, 1817, (ch. x, p. 111), where Miss Vernon says: "even *my* liberality cannot spare a gentleman above eight hours out of the twenty-four"; and in The Fair Maid of Perth, 1828, (ch. xv, p. 210): "Yet one word; — should a necessity occur for rousing yourself — for who in Scotland can promise himself eight hour's uninterrupted repose? — then smell the strong essence ..." The choice of the precise figure *eight* in these passages is certainly no magic, but no doubt derives ultimately from Alfred.

If we hunt for more precise references to Alfred and the eight hours we can find in Cobbett's writings of 1822 that, "King Alfred allowed eight hours for recreation in the twenty-four, eight for sleep, and eight for business. I did not take my allowance of the two former." (Cobbett, The Progress of a Ploughboy, ed. Reitzel, London 1933 p. 184). Lord Lytton has another reference to Alfred's division in Paul Clifford, 1830, (ch. xvi, p. 218): "What good man ever loves to be interrupted in his meditations? Even Alfred the Great could not bear it." Since 1830 Owen had toured the country lecturing on the necessity for his reforms, which included an eight hours' day. His Society for National Regeneration accepted the eight hours' day as an axiom (Cole, Attempts pp. 109, 137, 193). When, therefore, the eight hours' day crops up in fiction later than 1831 it may be derived from the general discussion and not from the Alfredian tradition. Thus in Disraeli's Sybil or the Two Nations (1845) we find (VI vi, p. 430): "we have a right to four shillings a day wages, eight hours' work and two pots of ale. — A fair day's wage for a fair day's work ...", and (p. 434—35), referring to the proposed National Holiday: "for all an enormous Sabbath, that was to compensate for any incidental suffering, which it induced by the increased means and the elevated condition that it ultimately would insure: that paradise of artisans, that Utopia of Toil, embalmed in those ringing words, sounds cheerful to the Saxon race: 'A fair day's wage for a fair day's work.'" [18] Here Disraeli betrays how little he actually felt for the labouring class whose interests he was virtually out to defend. In the dramatic and epic literature of the 18th and the beginning of 19th centuries, Alfred was such a popular theme that "England's darling" became a household word. It is said of Haydon, the painter, to whom Keats addressed two poems, that be had begun a portrait of King Alfred shortly before his death in 1846.

There are also other facts which testify to the popularity of this Anglo-Saxon King. In 1808 the Alfred Club was established in London, to be merged into the Oriental Club in 1855 (Cunningham, London Past and Present. I. 1891). As none of the records or books of any kind were taken over by the Oriental Club, according to a statement of its secretary in a letter of March 13, 1953, no information can be had from that quarter. According to Notes and Queries, 8th series (1892—7), vol. VI, pp. 208, 331, 377; and vol. VII, p. 136—7, it was amalgamated with the Oriental Club between 1852 and 1855, when some of its members joined the Athenaeum (see Ralph Nevill, London Clubs, 1911, pp. 283—84). It lost members over controversies on smoking and billiards, which the Athenaeum allowed. Lord Byron was a member in 1816, the only public figure remembered in connection with its social and literary record. He called it "a decent resource on a rainy day". Another member was James Mackintosh, and still another Richard Rush, the American minister, in 1818 (see A Residence of the Court of London. London 1833, p. 109). A correspondent has kindly informed me (in a letter of May 20, 1953), that the club was a dull sort of Tory resort, with some 17 bishops, and certainly had nothing whatever to do with social reform or the eight hours, or ten hours, agitation.

Still it is interesting to find a club, started in 1808, of the name of Alfred. What is more: during the period of 1810—1835 no less than five newspapers were issued under the name of Alfred. The first: The Alfred, Westminster Gazette. London, was a daily May 12, 1810—Dec. 31, 1810; and its (daily) continuation The Alfred. London, Jan.

---

[18] Also to be found in DICKENS, Our Mutual Friend, ch. 13, uttered by Eugene Wrayburn: "A fair day's wages for a fair day's work is ever my partner's motto." MAC COBY, The English Radical Tradition 1763—1914, London 1952, p. 138, records the expression in FEARGUS O'CONNOR's Letter to the working classes in the Northern Star, March 1. 1845. For the "normal working day", see p. 136 f. below.

1811—Dec. 31, 1811. The second was The Alfred. West of England
Journal And General Advertiser, Exeter, which was a weekly periodical.
There are seven volumes of it: I June 6, 1815—Dec. 30, 1817; II 1818
—20; III 1821—23; IV 1824—26; V 1827, 28, 29 (to May 26th);
VI June 2, 1829—Dec. 30, 1830; VII Jan. 1831—Aug. 1831. On
Sept. 6, 1831, this Exeter Alfred suddenly becomes The Exeter Inde-
pendent to Oct. 25, 1831. Also, by an odd process of duplication, it
becomes The Devonshire Chronicle and Exeter News (Jan. 1, 1831—
Dec. 25, 1831). The very first copy, June 6, 1815, has a 'banner' =
Aelfredus. magnus. rex. anglii, and a motto = Salus Populi, Suprema
Lex, and the Address reads as follows: "To promise, is light and easy
— to perform, often difficult. The Editor of the Alfred trusts that his
wishes will not run over in impotence, his promises be unperformed,
or his exertions want energy. The general character of his observations
shall wear as near a semblance, as his utmost efforts can produce, to
the end and motive of the actions of that great and venerable monarch,
whose name dignifies the title page. — At the name of ALFRED, the
heart of every true Briton will beat in rapture, as long as freedom shall
animate the sons of Albion. The political structure, raised by him, was
not an hapless compound of disjointed members, but a nicely organized
body, the minutest subdivision of which being touched, the whole
system vibrated. *The general will of the freemen was the centre* on
which it moved, and round which all the parts performed their func-
tions, without commotion, in well regulated harmony. The King, in the
midst of the circle, appeared as a fiduciary magistrate, accountable for
his actions, whenever the nation required it: and SALISBURY PLAIN
was the sacred spot on which the FOLKMOTE might assemble to
consider, revise, and correct the acts of the executive and legislative
powers. It was this effective principle, which was the soul of the
Constitution, and the guarantee of the people's rights; and where it
does not exist, the flame of liberty burns only by the sufferance of the
government. But in this most noble structure the slavery of the peasants
formed a murky stain, which all the power of the immortal ALFRED
could not immediately eradicate; but which would in time have been
effected by the energies of his institution, had not its main spring been
injured by succeeding princes. This was a Constitution so glorious, that
he would deserve the curse of Heaven, who, enjoying it(s) blessings,
would not shed his life's blood in its defence." In no. 846, Aug. 23,

1831, there is the following notice: "TO THE PUBLIC ... announces that, in consequence of a Weekly Journal having been recently started in London by the same title ... that the ALFRED, from and after the 20th instant, shall be called THE EXETER INDEPENDENT ..."

The Alfred. West of England Journal ... was a spirited journal, devoted to liberty in a strictly Whig manner. In June, 1816, it prints an election speech by a candidate (Mr. Tucker) who imputes to Alfred a state of things evidently regarded as a Golden Age. The paper discusses the distress of workers, etc., and shows compassion and sympathy. It often speaks with hatred of The Western Luminary, which, however, on Nov. 15, 1831, suddenly appears with this title: "Western Luminary and Family Newspaper. Exeter Independent. Late, Alfred", which runs to Dec. 20, 1831. Apparently there had been a fusion of the two antagonist papers. The spirit of the Exeter Alfred is, however, truly continued by The Taunton Courier and Western Advertiser (Jan.—Dec. 1832; Jan. 2—Dec. 1833). The third is The Intelligence, a weekly, which on July 31, 1831 re-names itself The Alfred. "We come before the public this week with a new name. We have chosen one which we hope not to disgrace, associated though it be with the proudest and fondest feelings of every English patriot. Courageous without rashness, wise without ostentation, a reformer but not a destroyer, a lover of justice, but a respecter of the rights, usages, and customs of the people, the name of ALFRED awakens recollections which forbid the entertainment of unworthy or unpatriotic motives." (July 31— Dec. 25, 1831; Jan. 1— Dec. 30, 1832; Jan. 1— April, 1833). From this Alfred appears to come some of the matter for two provincial papers, The Alfred, London Weekly Journal and Bridgewater and Somersetshire General Advertiser (Aug. 10—Dec. 19, 1831; Jan. 2— Dec. 31, 1832; Jan. 7—Dec. 30, 1833); and The Blackburn Alfred, a weekly (Aug. 6—Dec. 31, 1832; Jan. 7—Dec. 25, 1833; Jan. 1—Dec. 31, 1834; and Jan. 7, 1835). On Jan. 28, 1835, it is followed by The Blackburn Standard (until Dec. 30, 1835), which states that it continues all that was valuable in the Alfred.

There is a good deal in all the papers about the factory children, about petitions of starving weavers, about the ten-hour bill, etc. There are many incidents between 1830 and 1833 sympathetically reported. Alfred was remembered, primarily, for the sake of his virtues, and he became known to everybody, also to the illitterate, as a patriot king and a social reformer. The Alfredian division of the day and night was not considered to be practical politics even by Radicals (cf. Place: p. 126, footn. 23; Cole, Attempts p. 153). But pioneering spirits tasted more deeply the Alfredian spring and saw in a flash the importance of this Anglo-Saxon monarch's (supposed) rule.

It is impossible to agree with Lord Passfield that to relate King Alfred's threefold division of the day with the latter-day claim for an eight-hour working day by the Labour movement is merely fanciful. The tradition among the workmen, if there was any, that eight hours was a just proportion of the twenty-four hours to assign to work, must have originated in the Alfredian tradition. We opened chapter III by pointing out that it is problematic whether William of Malmesbury invented the threefold division of the day, which he ascribed to King Alfred. And now, workmen and Radicals had hit upon exactly the same division! In all other countries of the western world the idea of limiting the working day to eight hours had never been thought of, — yet in England twice! With all respect to Messrs Webb and Cox, in referring to the rhyme they quote, which they say to be of Australian origin, they show that they had never intended to investigate the matter seriously from a historical point of view. The Encyclopaedia of Social Sciences says that "legend attributes to King Alfred the saying: 'Eight hours work, eight hours sleep, eight hours play, make a just and healthy day!' This is, of course, unhistoric, but shows how lightheartedly one may deal with truth. J. A. Froude's Oceana (1886, p. 209) notes, concerning his visit to New Zealand, among other things that: "Meanwhile it was the workman's paradise. The four eights, that ideal of operative felicity, are here a realised fact." (Ref. in a footnote): "Eight to work, eight to play, eight to sleep, and eight shillings a day." In a letter to the editor of The Observer in the early 1930's one Mr A. H. Williams writes: "When I was a boy at school in New Zealand, in the late 'seventies, the jingle

> Eight hours' work,
> Eight hours' play,
> Eight hours' sleep,
> And eight bob a day,

was a slogan commonly used by the 'working' classes at parliamentary elections in New Zealand." It is evident, as Messrs Webb and Cox say,

that the last line points to an Australasian origin. What's what in the
Labour Movement (compiled by Waldo R. Browne, New York 1921)
gives under the heading Three Eights the explanation: "Denotes the
working-class ideal of a day divided into three equal periods of eight
hours each — one period for work, another for play, and the third for
sleep."[19] The same source says under the heading Eight Hour Day:
". . . In general, what is known as the 'eight hour movement' has reference to a working day actually limited to eight hours. Those who support this movement are merely endeavouring to restore a condition that
existed in the 15th and 16th centuries — as Thorold Rogers and other
labor historians have clearly shown. In the 17th century working hours
began to lengthen, until a working day of fifteen hours, even for
children, became by no means uncommon." This unhistoric statement
based mainly on Thorold Rogers is interesting because once again it
shows that when a political, or labour, reform is proposed in England,
the reformers often prefer to dig up some old law, or custom, or precedent to support the claim instead of demonstrating that hygiene,
reason, justice, changed conditions, modern technique, or some such
cause demands a change of legislation. (Cf. Macaulay, History of England. I pp. 27—29; Trevelyan, English Social History 96.)

According to prevailing ideas workmen were not able to take care
of their leisure; it was best for them to work all through most of the
twenty-four hours. Bishop Berkeley had once declared that work was
in itself *voluptas* for Irish farmers, and the upper classes had the same
opinion about their British labouring people. Still some of the masters
understood that the labour policy carried out by employers was radi-

---

[19] Modern paraphrases on the Labour jingle of the division of the day are the
American: "Lucky, lucky, lucky me, / I am a lucky son of a gun, / I work eight
hours, I sleep eight hours, / I have eight hours of fun" (a dance tune of 1952); an
anti-Labour parody: "Work eight hours and don't worry. Then you may become a boss
and work sixteen hours a day and have all the worry"; and the British: "Not a penny
off the pay, Not a minute on the day," (during the General Strike in 1926); and the
American of 1945: "Fifty-two for forty or fight," meaning pay for fifty-two hours
for a working week of forty hours, or strike! See also What's What in the Labor
Movement: Forty-Four Hour Week; Forty-Hour Week; Short Hour Movement: "As
the common ideal of labor has long been a working day limited to eight hours (for,
it is said, the organized effort, beginning in England early in the nineteenth century
. . . to secure a shorter working day), the 'short hour movement' and the 'eight hour
movement' are or until recently have been largely synonymous."

cally wrong. But they had a long way to go before they achieved something, though. Foremost among them were John Fielden of Todmorden,
John Wood of Bradford, Rathbone Greg, Richard Oastler, and — of
course — Robert Owen. As is well-known Owen started from a humble
station of life, but already at twenty he was manager of a mill with
500 operatives, and a few years later manager (and later still the biggest
shareholder) of the New Lanark mills which employed 2.500 operatives.
He must have been a very astute director and businessman, and had
he devoted his time to money-making he might have become one of the
wealthiest men in Britain, which in those days was equivalent to saying
of the world. But there ran in him a streak of philantropy very excep-
tional among the masters, and among the educated men of his time.
Since he was a shrewd businessman he was able to give reasons for his
pro-Labour ideas. First of all he wanted to reduce the hours of child
labour. In his writings (A New View of Society. 1812—13, and others)
he mentions that children from six to sixteen worked 14, 15 and even
18 hours a day, all the time *indoors*, and compares this state of affairs
with conditions thirty years earlier when they generally did not begin
until they were fourteen. (But Owen himself began at nine!) The bill
Sir Robert Peel brought before Parliament in 1815 had been drawn up
by Owen. There he wanted to fix maximum hours of child labour at
10 hours for boys and girls above 12; under 12 children might be
allowed to work in such branches where tiny workers were required,
but then for only six hours a day until the age of 12. In his letter On
the Employment of Children in Manufactories (A New View ...
p. 137), addressed to the Prime Minister, the Earl of Liverpool, in 1818
he further suggests: "And no manufacturer should be permitted to
employ either young or old for a longer period than twelve hours per
day, allowing them out of that time one hour for breakfast and another
for dinner, leaving ten hours for full and constant work, which is one
more than our ancestors thought beneficial(!); and I doubt whether
nine hours of regular and active employment, established as the
measure of daily labour to be required from the working classes, would
not be still more economical and profitable for the country." Owen
looked at economic factors with the eyes of a political economist plus
those of a philantropist. He could not conform to the idea that gain
was the only motive behind industrial activity: the employer had duties
to the country, not only in paying taxes but also in caring for the

human beings he controlled, and so indirectly, for national health. In his concern for saving man-power and keeping workers fit and healthy, Owen became an educator: even here one might say that he was guided by business principles. For if the children were given regular education in schools and time to play in the open air in healthful surroundings, and were not enslaved in factories at an early age, there would grow up a healthy race, excellent recruits for the factories and other jobs, working lesser hours but producing more than the feeble wretches who then worked longer hours. Vice and poverty would diminish and die out, the poor rates could be reduced,[20] a programme still to be fully realised in western Europe. It is a marvel how Owen managed to reform his own New Lanark mill community, how he found time for his missionary zeal for bettering labour conditions, and how his undertaking made him and his shareholders richer.

We have seen that Owen recommended six hours' work a day for children under twelve when required for special jobs. But on one occasion he mentioned the figure 8 as a reasonable number of working hours. This was in connection with his pet scheme for communal villages run by mutual cooperation, derived possibly from Spence's parishes[21] and from his New Lanark system, later to be realized in his American model colony New Harmony, which collapsed after a few years. In the accompanying volume to Owen's Life written by Himself, or Volume 1 A (London 1858), which contains "A Series of Reports, Addresses, etc., 1808—1820", we find (p. 90) a "Letter published in the London Newspaper of August 9th, 1817". In it Owen contrasts the regrettable conditions in the manufacturing towns with the 'happy villages', which he had been proposing for a great number of years: "In the manufacturing towns — the parents must toil from ten to sixteen hours in the day to procure the wretched subsistence ... In the proposed villages — the parents will be healthfully and pleasantly occupied not more than eight hours in the day." *Eight hours in the day!* This was written by a well-read man, and so there cannot be the slightest

---

[20] Unemployed subsisting on the rich, see OWEN, Relief for the Poor 159. — Description of the villages, see OWEN, Relief for the Poor p. 180; idem, Letters on Poor Relief 214—5, 218—9, 222; idem, Plan for the Relief of the Poor 227. Cf. SOUTHEY's (more or less) wholehearted support of OWEN's social programme: Colloquies I 62, 132, 144; II 420.

[21] See O. R. RUDKIN, Thomas Spence and his Connections. 1927, p. 70; 180 ff.; 191.

doubt that Owen was influenced by the Alfredian tradition, especially if we remember how poets and historians had glorified King Alfred, and how many of them had described his threefold division of the day.

About 1830 it is possible to distinguish between two distinct trends: one fighting for an eight hours' day, another — more reasonable, as it was said — for a ten hours' day.[22] Owen, Doherty, and Fielden represented the eight hours programme in 1831: "the new powers of production were amply great enough to enable all the world's work to be done in a day of not more than eight hours" (Cole I 117). One of the basic axioms of the Owenite Society for National Regeneration, adopted on November 25, 1833, ran: "Eight hours' daily labour is enough for any human being ..." (Maccoby 104); the eight hours' day was to begin from March 1, 1834 (Maccoby 107). This proposal led to the abortive strike of the Lancashire cotton operatives for an eight hours' day (Webb 158).[23] The tailors in London, who had been most energetic at the great

[22] Cf. the remarkable statement in THOMAS p. 63 f.: "The extent to which the advocates of the ten-hours bill were really interested in the welfare of the children whose cause they pleaded so vehemently was illustrated by the amendment, moved by Brotherton (1833), that children under thirteen should work not for eight, but for ten hours a day, since this would be better for masters and operatives". Thomas adds: "The Government, who in this respect at least had stolen the thunder of the reformers, opposed this suggestion, and carried the House with them." Cf. also ibid. p. 87; COLE, Attempts, pp. 79—80.

[23] WEBB, History of Trade Unionism 156, quotes Francis Place: "The nonsensical doctrines preached by Robert Owen and others respecting communities and goods in common; abundance of everything man ought to desire, and all for four hours' labour out of every twenty-four; the right of every man to his share of the earth in common, and his right to whatever his hands had been employed upon; the power of masters under the present system to give just what wages they pleased; the right of the labourer to such wages as would maintain him and his in comfort for eight or ten hours' labour;" etc. I have not been able to find that Owen ever proposed four hours' work a day. Place was thoroughly disgusted at Owen's new departure and that may well account for his bad humour. Cf. also AXEL GJÖRES, Robert Owen, Stockholm 1932, p. 135, showing Place's intense dislike of Owen's fantastic social planning. — WEBB, loc. cit. 132, records Doherty carrying on the agitation for an eight hours day (1833). "The plan is (writes J. Fielden to W. Cobbett) that ... the said Bill (now Act) limits the time of Work for children under eleven years of age to eight hours a day, those above that age, both grown persons and adults, should insist on eight hours a day being the maximum of time for them to labour ..." — WEBB, loc. cit. 151: "The Cotton Spinners ... preparing (1834) to carry out Fielden's idea of a general strike for an eight hours day — resolved to demand the reduction of hours from 1 April 1834 ... limiting the hours of children

demonstration protesting against the sentence of the Tolpuddle labourers on April 21st, 1834, found a middle way only four days later by demanding a ten hours' day at 6 shillings during the summer and an eight hours' day at 5 shillings during the rest of the year. (Maccoby 110.) Many workmen were themselves a little afraid of a radical reduction of hours from the current 15, 14 or 12 to the ideal 8. Richard Oastler, the 'Throne and Altar' Tory who was to devote his life and fortune to the cause of labour, found a more reasonable transition in limiting the hours to 10. Maccoby (p. 34) writes that in 1831 the Yorkshire woollen districts were organising the Factory Ten Hours Movement, which led on to the 1833 Factory bill. That bill, the first to pass the reformed Parliament, prescribed a minimum age of nine years for entrants into the textile factories and also a maximum working day of nine hours, or a working week of 48 hours, for children below the age of thirteen, and prohibited night work by young persons. Inspectors were to see that the law was observed. The working day for adult workers remained the same and agitation among the workers for shorter hours continued.

It is interesting to record the various opinions of the day concerning the proper number of working hours and the possible reduction of hours with a view to Parliament and legislation. In a letter to Oastler in 1831 Sir John Cam. Hobhouse regretted that Sadler, the member for Aldborough, had appeared to favour ten hours of daily labour for five days and eight on the Saturday — "nothing can be more idle" (Alfred I 139). Sadler's passionate plea for his bill "for regulating the labour of children and young persons in the mills and factories" in the House of Commons on March 16, 1832, is an important document. (Alfred I 151 ff.) I forgo all the details of the description of the sweating system, only stress the information given on the number of hours for various categories. The country labourers had an average of

---

to eight per day." — Webb, loc. cit. 136: "the riotous demand for an eight hours day at Oldham in 1834". Cf. also DRIVER, Tory Radical pp. 261 (8 hours' work in the whole country) —265; 315—6; 535; THOMAS p. 56 footn. 31: extreme reformers were pressing for an eight hours' day for adults (1833). THOMAS quotes a Catechism of the Society for Promoting National Regeneration (1833): "What ought to be the Maximum of Time for daily labour?" — "Eight hours a day — or from eight o'clock in the morning till midday, and from two o'clock in the afternoon till six o'clock in the evening ..." New light on the period is given by COLE, Attempts 81 f., 109, 137, 193.

9

eight or nine hours of actual work throughout the year (ibid. 196). Every prisoner sentenced to hard labour had to be employed so many hours a day, not exceeding ten, exclusively of the time allowed for meals, according to the law, but Sadler had found that the average labour fell far short of these limits. The convicts at the hulks worked in summer 9 hours and in winter about two hours less (ibid. 197 f.). Slaves worked no more than 9 hours a day (ibid. 198). The outcome of all the dissensions between the reformers was that the Ten-Hour Day was accepted as politically possible to realize. There was an enormous propaganda among the workers for this measure. Thus, in Manchester in 1832, Sadler and Oastler were greeted by the crowd singing, 'Sadler for ever, Oastler for ever; six in the morning, six in the evening' (ibid. 255). In Leeds, in 1833, at a mass meeting (ibid. II 46) the factory children sang in unison,.

> We will have the Ten Hours Bill,
> That we will — that we will;
> Or the land shall ne'er be still,
> We will have the Ten Hours Bill.

The slogan, the Ten-Hour Day, also entered literature. In Mrs. Frances Trollope's novel Michael Armstrong, The Factory Boy (1840; p. 206) Mr Bell, the clergyman says, "All that we ask for, ... all that the poor people ask for themselves, is that by Act of Parliament it should be rendered illegal for men, women and children to be kept to the wearying unhealthy labour of the mills for more than ten hours out of every day, leaving their daily wages at the same rate as now." In the campaign one notices, however, that sometimes there was a threatening attitude of some short-time committees; Alfred (II 106 f.) records the resolution of one in 1836: "But we have *not* got, and they say we shall never have the Ten Hours' Bill. We say we will either have *that*, or something else, a great deal *more*, and a good deal *better* — and what say *you*?" Alfred adds: "The 'something better', referred to was expressed in a resolution of the central committee, asking the factory operatives to offer their opponents the alternative of the adults ceasing to work with the children at the close of eight hours, or the parliament enacting a ten hours' factory law."[24]

[24] See also MACCOBY 174—5, 236, 249, 255, 266, 272—3; 401, 406; WEBB, History of Trade Unionism 188, 190.

Thus to say that the eight hours' day was far from the minds of the labouring class is wrong. Why Oastler and others pressed for a ten hours' day was that it was a political measure that could be realized at a point not too far distant. To have pressed for an eight hours' day would have been in vain at the time. But when the Radicals kept propagating incessantly for the ten hours' day and many of them pooh-poohed Owen and his sometimes nonsensical ideas, it is easy to understand why the idea of an eight hours' day was relegated to the lumber-room and almost forgotten, except as a memory of Dreamland.[25]

After many vicissitudes the Bill of 1847 fixed the number of hours at ten per day: it limited the daily work of women and youths in textile mills, and because of that the masters could not force the men to continue, since the work could not be carried on by them alone: "The period between 1825 and 1848 was remarkable for the frequency and acuteness of its commercial depression", write the Webbs (p. 180). "From 1850 industrial expansion was for many years both greater and steadier than many previous periods." The British workmen, who considered themselves cheated by the Reform of 1832, because they were still denied the franchise, had entered upon a period of class struggle, strikes, risings, and organisations, but all were premature. The Spinners' National Union of 1829, led by Doherty, Owen's Society for National Regeneration, the Chartists,[26] and several trade unions, advocated shorter hours, but there was no general, nation-wide organisation, with funds and other resources, to support the claims of the workers. This is well reflected in the fiction of the day, such as Disraeli's Sybil and Mrs. Gaskell's Mary Barton, where the Chartist congresses, their internal dissensions, their optimism and want of strength to back up their threats are aptly described. In Sybil (II xiii, p. 133) there is recorded: "Twelve hours of daily labour at the rate of one penny an hour for a handloom weaver"; and in Mary Barton (ch. viii, p. 85)

---

[25] The Oastler papers, "Oastler & The Factory Movement 1830—35" — a collection of broadsides, contained in a volume in the University of London Library, as well as the collection of Oastler papers in the British Museum (Add. 41748), do naturally not refer to the 8 hours' day in any way. — FRANCES E. GILLESPIE's Labor and Politics in England 1850—1867 (Duke Univ. Pr. 1927) has not a single, however unimportant, reference to the demand for an 8 hours' day, which was voiced, though, now and then in that period.

[26] Cf. MAC COBY, The English Radical Tradition 1763—1914, p. 137.

John Barton while reading the Northern Star comments: "There's the right stuff in this here Star, and no mistake. Such a right-down piece for short hours." — "At the same rate of wages as now?" asked Jem. — "Aye, aye! else where's the use? ..."[27]; and (p. 89): "for my part", said a shivering, half-clad man who crept near the fire, as if ague-stricken," would like thee to tell 'em (at the Chartist meeting) to pass th' Short-Hours Bill. Flesh and blood gets wearied wi' so much work ..." In the same novel (p. 86) a doctor declares "that by far th' greater o' the accidents as camed in, happened in th' last two hours o' work, when folk getten tired and careless". In 1848 the Labour League newspaper demanded 'regulation of the hours of labour in all trades, with a view to equalise and diffuse employment'. (Maccoby 403.)

The Chartists failed in 1848, when they intended to deliver a petition signed by more than five million Englishmen to the Government. The Government saw through the strength of the movement realizing that Chartism was a weak, feeble, wavering body, and felt itself stronger than before. A feeling of failure spread among the supporters of the movement.

We shall now shift the scene to Australia. After the liberation of the American colonies Australia had been found to be a suitable country for transported convicts. But side by side with this emigration of white people under duress to the island continent, which was stopped in the 1840's, there had been a voluntary emigration of land-owners, workmen and tradesmen, and the various colonies developed at a remarkable rate. In 1851 gold discoveries were made in the colony of Victoria, not so far from Melbourne, and in the same year the township of Ballarat was founded as a centre of the golddigging crowds, — of which we get a glimpse in Henry Handel Richardson's novel The Fortune of Richard Mahony I: Australia Felix. "Finally came the remarkable gold discoveries in Australia in 1851", writes Maccoby (p. 363), "which sent a veritable gold-fever through the veins even of men (in Great Britain) who had been brooding on social wrongs in 1839, 1842, and 1848. In 1852 alone 87.881 persons left the United Kingdom for Australasia, and then ports like Sunderland saw direct emigrant sailing to the Southern Seas. A number of Manchester Chartists, meanwhile, were hoping to form a considerable party to sail with

---

[27] Cf. THOMAS p. 176.

Dr. M'Douall, the fiery 'physical force' orator of 1839, the would-be revolutionary leader of 1842 and the sedition convict of 1848—50. M'Douall's departure in 1853 to seek in Australia the professional competence he had never won in England is no inept reminder of the steady drain on democratic combativeness which emigration had long been making."

An Australian, W. E. Murphy, author of History of the Eight Hour Movement (Melbourne 1896), met several of the Chartists, for (p. 21) he says: "It has been my good fortune to have met on terms of personal intimacy many of the old Chartists in London, and while 'on tramp' through the provinces of the United Kingdom. Here in Australia I have enjoyed the friendship of an excellent few who carried their old principles well to the forefront in an honest endeavour to solve the problem of how best to secure the greatest good to the greatest number." This obvious reference to Jeremy Bentham, who represented Reason without any sentimental bias, does not prevent Murphy from romanticizing about the first introduction of the 8 hours' day in Australasia. He does not believe in the Alfredian tradition as the root of this special number of hours for the simple reason that in Alfred's days there was no 8 hours' day! But he knows about Owen's suggestion in 1831, and then his theory of the origin of the day is unveiled. He believes in the magic of the figure 8 and refers to some such fatuities as that "the people's charter was promulgated in the *eight* month ... by *eight* men" (p. 12), or that the New Zealand Company in 1840 divided its income into $^3/_8$, $^2/_8$, $^1/_8$, and $^2/_8$ for various items (p. 14). (One might as well refer to the fact that the Cobden propaganda was started by the Eight Men of Manchester. G. L.) The Company just mentioned was, according to Murphy, responsible for the introduction of the eight hours' day in New Zealand, for (p. 15) some of the colonists suggested its introduction in the charter, but to this was objected that "the latter clause would be inoperative, as contracts to bind free settlers to serve under any conditions of labour beyond the sea was not provided for by any Imperial statute". In 1847 the Rev. Thomas Burns arrived to present-day Dunedin in whose neighbourhood was Bell Hill. Murphy continues (p. 16): "From this eminence, amidst the sound of the axes of the woodmen and the swish of the break saws, as they drove through the green forest trees, the measure of *Eight Hours* as the toiler's limit in the New World *first* reverberated through the dense New Zealand bush — the harbinger of those brighter days which at last dispelled with glorious realisation — the dream of ages." (!)

Thus, to Murphy, the 8 hours' day was not the result of trade union preparation, but to "that true elixir of economic science the virtue of mutual concession" (p. 18). At the end of 1848 the N. Z. Company, which had then accepted the name of The Otago Association, demanded 9 and even 10 hours' work from the settlers. A meeting of settlers was called, protested against the demand and carried a resolution embodying the 8 hours' day. A newcomer from Britain, Mr. Valpey, who had acquired a large estate in New Zealand, offered work to the settlers on the 8 hours' basis, and the Association had to give in in 1849 (p. 19). The settlers were mostly Scotch. This is Murphy's relation, but he does not say whether the 8 hours' day continued to exist. He only says (p. 36) that bad harvest years and the gold discoveries in Australia caused "the first blight on the corporate efforts of the Presbyterian projectors to retain as a system the Eight Hours' Day". The Company was dissolved in 1850. André Siegfried, Neu-Seeland (Germ. ed., Berlin 1909) does not mention this romantic story, nor does he say that the eight hours' day ever existed, but on p. 80 he refers to a statute of the 1870's prescribing 8 hours' work for women. The leading spirit of the New Zealand Company was Edward Gibbon Wakefield (1796—1862). He was the grandson of Priscilla Wakefield (1751—1832), philantropist and author, the son of Edward Wakefield (1774—1854), political economist and land-agent, the nephew of Daniel Wakefield (1776—1846), political economist and barrister, and brother of Felix Wakefield (1807 —75), engineer and colony organiser. That Edward Gibbon Wakefield, after a stormy career in his youth, became an able expert on colonisation and to-day is termed one of the makers of the Empire, is not to be denied. But whether he was interested in a reform of the length of the working hours is not known. Murphy's story seems more sentimental than based on facts.

Far more important is Murphy's description of how the 8 hours' day became a fact in Australia. He mentions four names, Thomas Walter Vine, a London carpenter and a Chartist in London, arrived in Victoria in 1853; James Stephens, a Welsh stonemason and Chartist of some standing in London, arrived in Melbourne in 1855; James Gilvra from Scotland, and Benjamin Douglass from Kent, arrived in Melbourne in 1855. In Melbourne the working-hours had previously been 10 or more.

Hugh Laundry, of the Operative Stonemasons' Society of New South Wales in Sydney, moved on September 22, 1855 "That in the opinion of this Society Eight Hours should be the maximum of a day's labour", which was seconded by Thomas Eaves and carried unanimously. The employers gave in at once. In Melbourne, on February 4, 1856, James Stephens moved the introduction of the 8 hours' day, and on February 18, 1856, he supported his case with facts and figures. On the very same day the motion was carried. (Murphy pp. 32—49.) Even here the employers speedily accepted the conditions of the workers.

Now, in 1856 the Eight Hours' Day was realized in Australia. Its connection with British traditions goes without saying. The Chartist *emigrés* certainly vented their ideas on arriving in Australia. J. T. Sutcliffe, in A History of Trade Unionism in Australia (Melbourne 1921), states (p. 23 f.) that "previously (to the gold discoveries) the standard of labour in England had been the practical test of the condition of these (working) classes in Australia. After the gold era, the wages standard and also the standard of living, were fixed generally without reference to the standard of other countries ... The rush to the goldfields had depleted the few established industries of the labour required to work them, and so it came about that, in towns especially, all classes of labour were in great demand and, as we have seen, wages rose to a phenomenal figure. It is to this fact that the establishment of the eight hour day, that great charter of the early Trade Unionism of Australia, owes its origin. The records are at variance as to whether Sydney or Melbourne can claim to be the first place in which recognition of the eight hour day was secured. In both places it was first granted to the stone masons." Now it was exactly within the English building trade that the eight hour day claim was raised. According to an article in the Australian Worker, Sept. 30, 1915, a number of masons from London had been engaged for the building of the parliament house in Sydney, "men who had taken advantage of their sojourn in London to attend classes for improving themselves, both mentally and vocationally". In 1855, after a few months' stay in Australia, they found their work too severe and exacting in the Australian climate, and they decided to agitate for shorter hours. After a conference between employers and workmen the Eight Hours' Day was recognized and put into practice on April 21, 1856. This Short Hours Day spread all over Australia, though not in all trades. The account given by Webb and

Cox (1891, p. 38) amounts to practically the same. The Eight Hours Movement began in 1856 in Melbourne. Already in 1853, during the abortive strike in the building trade in London, there was general talk about the adventges of an eight hours' day, and Webb supposes that some emigrants brought the idea with them to Australia. An Eight Hours League was formed at a meeting of the various trade unions; their resolution, immediately communicated to the public, provided that after April 21, 1856, no one, being a member of those organisations, should work more than eight hours. There was no chance of resistance on the part of the masters, and after three weeks of agitation the rule was agreed to and has since remained in force. — Sutcliffe, loc. cit., says that ever since 1871 the Eight Hours Day is annually celebrated in Sydney, and that the birthday of it in Melbourne is April 21 (from 1856). Webb and Cox say that there is general holiday on April 22. — Cronqvist, a Swedish emigrant to Australia, writes in Vandringar i Australien 1857—1859 (p. 13): "the eight-hours-system ('eight-hours-association')" was introduced in Melbourne, according to which a workman "works eight hours, allots eight hours to pleasure, and reposes eight hours of the twenty-four". — Knös, another Swedish emigrant, writes in Bilder ur Lifvet i Australien (1875) that 'the 8 hours' demonstration' (p. 219) is a grand festival, celebrated by all the unions of workmen. It begins with a solemn procession. Every union was proceded by one or more banners, which all bore the common device: 8 hours' work, 8 hours' repose, 8 hours' diversion.

If we do not accept the supposition that the root of the Australasian 8 hours' day is to be found in England, we should consequently be forced to believe that yet another time, the third, the idea of the equity of 8 hours' work a day developed in an Anglo-Saxon community, which sounds incredible.

In the U. S. A., according to Philip S. Foner (History of the Labor Movement in the United States. New York 1947; pp. 98—101), the working hours between 1820—30 were 'from sun to sun', or fourteen and a half, including $1\frac{1}{2}$ for meals, which meant 13 hours actual work; he records, however, (p. 118), that skilled workers had achieved a 10 hours' day in 1835, and from then on there was a gradual reduction. In 1829 a play, The Banks of Hudson; or the Congress Trooper by Thomas Dibdin was performed in London. There occurs a slave song: "We worky for massa ... From rising de sun Til daylight be done ..." In 1836 (19 Nov.) the National Laborer newspaper wrote (Foner 363): "We have no desire to perpetuate the ten hour system, for we believe that eight hours daily labor is more than enough for any man to perform." This seems to be an echo of Owen's propaganda. In 1851 there was a mass-meeting in New York declaring that "eight hours is a just and sufficient number of hours for any man to work". James Truslow Adams writes in The Epic of America that in certain factories, especially Lowell's, the working conditions were considered to be excellent in those days (1800—1820), but they got worse in the 1830's. Working hours were generally from 5 a.m. to 7 p.m. Female workers were required to live in the factory tenements, and some kind of patriarchal system developed, so that they had to go to bed at a certain hour, go to church on Sundays, and even to a certain church. They knew no personal liberty. About 1845 the middle states had accepted a 9 hours day in several trades, but in New England they kept to twelve or fourteen hours a day. One reason for this was the 18th century one: the moral character of the factory hands would suffer if they were away for a long period of hours from the wholesome discipline of the factories, and dissipation, crime, wickedness, and pauperism would follow. (Foner 199—201.) The socalled Ten-Hour Philosophy, on the other hand, argued that also workmen ought to have time enough to think and cultivate their souls. The difference between the middle states and New England must be explained as in the case of Australia by the shortage of man-power in the west. The Ten-Hour propaganda among the workers went on into the 1860's, which indicates that American employers did not give in as easily as the English ones. The Baltimore Convention (the word 'convention' was borrowed from the English Chartists) of 1866 called on President Andrew Jackson to demand an eight hours' day. They justified their demands for it by maintaining that a threefold division of the twenty-four hours: 8 for work, 8 for repose, recreation and studies, and 8 for sleep was 'natural'. In 1868 Congress voted the Eight-Hours Day for all workers in federal employ (Foner 377). In 1884 there was an intense campaign for a general eight-hours' day in Chicago, according to Louis Adamic (Dynamite. The Story of Class Violence in America. New York 1931; p. 62); late in the year 1885 an Eight-Hour Association was formed in America.

If we turn back to Great Britain we shall see that there had been a

tendency to reduce hours still further,[28] but it began earlier than in the
American states. Already in 1853 the building operatives in London
began to claim 9 hours a day, and in 1867 the masons of the North-
East Coast struck for 'Nine Hours' (Cole II 67); at the beginning of
the 'seventies the Nine Hours Movement was in full swing. When the
Eight Hours' Day movement was growing in importance, the Daily
News wrote on July 13, 1897: "A nine-hour day is not so long as to
be exhausting to a man." But the ideal of eight hours was not forgotten. In 1867 at a meeting of Lancashire textile operatives, presided over
by the Rev. J. R. Stephens, a resolution embodied the following
demand: "to agitate for such a measure of legislative restriction as shall
secure a uniform Eight Hours Bill in factories, exclusive of meal-times,
for adults, females, and young persons, and that such Eight Hours Bill
have for its foundation a restriction on the moving power." (Webb,
History of Trade Unionism p. 309; cf. pp. 309—92.) Names such as
Eight-Hour Law and Eight-Hour Movement turn up as early as 1869
although the working classes themselves were not always agreed on the
advisability of asking for an Eight-Hour Day.[29] In 1867 Marx published
his first volume of Das Kapital, which set people thinking. It was a
great incitement to reformers, and the concentrated reports on the
wrongs suffered by the labouring classes in England during the centuries
caused a sensation even among international Socialists. It must be
admitted, though, that Marx had found his arguments mostly in the
reports compiled by the factory inspectors, and, for earlier ages, from
historical works by Englishmen. "What is a working-day?" asks Marx,
and then proceeds to give pictures of the life of slavery led by English
workmen. In the eighth chapter we find a theoretical investigation into
the matter: work cannot be continued above a certain maximum limit.
This maximum is doubly defined. On the one hand by the physical
limitation of a man's power to work. A human being can render only a
certain portion of labour during the twenty-four hours of the natural
day. A horse cannot do more than eight hours work daily over a period
of time. For some time during the day man must recuperate, at other

---

[28] STEFFEN III p. 74 (ch. 29) gives a good picture of the decreasing trend of the
working hours in 1830—90.

[29] STEFFEN, Brittiska Ströftåg (1895; pp. 58—59) says that two Labour delegates,
Charles Fenwick and Thomas Burt, were against the enactment of an eight hour's day
for miners; probably the miners then worked less than 8 hours.

times man has other physical cravings: to eat, wash or dress. This theory had been expressed by Comenius, the Czech pedagogue of the 17th century. Marx introduced the term 'the normal working day', but he leaves us in the dark as to its length. And quite right, too, for it would have been dangerous to fix the labourer's and factory hand's working-day at eight hours a day for ever. Martin Buber, Paths in Utopia (London 1949, p. 85) reminds us that in 1864, in the Inaugural Address to the International Workers' Association, Marx praised the Ten-Hour-Law as the "triumph of principle". The word "the normal working day', however, stuck in the arguments of the reformers — but is not to be found in The New English Dictionary. Apparently it had no definite sense as to the length of the working day in Marx's days. Dr. Thomas uses it twice (pp. 318, 327) in his book; on my asking him for an explanation of the term, Dr. Thomas kindly replied in a letter dated Oct. 3, 1952: "It seems to me that in these early days the workers had no pre-conceived notion as to what constituted a fair day's work — they were rather concerned to secure *some* reduction, and were compelled to press the claims of the protected classes in order that they themselves might benefit by implication as it were. The 'normal' day was not the 'ideal' day, but rather a day in which all started and stopped at the same time in order to make relays impossible. Thus the word has a somewhat specialised meaning in this context." 'The normal working day' has, then, a rather elastic sense which may denote different things in various ages. This is also borne out in Steffen's booklet, Normalarbetsdagen. (Stockholm 1907). Finally, as we all know, the international congresses during the 1880's, especially that of 1889 in Paris, demanded a maximum eight hours' daily work, and workers agitated for this claim on every May-Day from 1890 onwards.

There are at least two historical theses for the doctorate on this subject in French: Maurice Noël, La limitation des heures de travail (Angers 1907), and François Baixès, La journée de 8 heures en France (Perpignan 1911). They are interesting in that both stress the fact that the eight hours' day is an English idea, an English invention. Noël gives us (p. 9) an *exposé* of the working hours in Ancient Greece, and from Rome he quotes: Servi pro nullis habentur. Servile caput nullum jus habet; (p. 15) he records an Ordonnance by the provost of Paris, May 12, 1395: work from sunrise to sunset, meals included; (p. 23) there was a tendency to increase the working hours in the 15th and the 16th centuries; actual increase in the 17th and 18th centuries (p. 26), but on the other hand the numerous religious holidays made the workers tolerate the worse conditions with regard to hours (p. 28). The French Revolution is an instance of how little the upper classes cared about working time, since no regulation was issued about that (p. 40—42); the author quotes the English jingle about the four 8's (work play, sleep, shillings) and goes on to say that the French miners at Courrières demanded also the four 8's (8 francs instead of 8 shillings) after a catastrophe in that mine (p. 327). — Baixès mentions (p. 9) that the first time an act about eight hours a day in industry was legislated was on March 22, 1841, restricting work for children of eight years of age in the factories. Working time was until 1848 very long in the textile industry: 15 to 15 ½ hours a day, generally varying between 14 and 18 hours a day (p. 13). The decree of March 2, 1848, limited the hours to 10 in Paris, 11 in the province (p. 19). He admits that the eight hours' day is an English idea. Finally, here is a quotation from Francois Coppée, Franc Parler. I. 1894 p. 176: "Sans compter, o monsieur Aulard, que le sansculotte Jésus, comme l'appelait Camille Desmoulins, fut, en fait de socialisme, un illustre précurseur, et que la parabole des ouvriers de la dernière heure est autrement radicale que la théorie des trois-huit." "Les trois-huit" was the slogan for a reform regarding working hours in France.

As has been pointed out above, in no period of the history of man has a threefold division of the twenty-four hours been thought of, except in England. It is quite unique. We know that William of Malmesbury ascribed this division to King Alfred the Great (d. 900), and he expressly said that Alfred had himself divided the natural day in that way. We have seen how the Alfredian tradition lived on to about 1830, a time when Alfred was celebrated by the poets as a champion of freedom and a liberal legislator, and a time when the demand for a maximum of eight hours' daily work was being voiced by the workmen of Britain, yea, even later. We have seen how the first Eight-Hours' Day was agreed to in a British colony in 1856, in Australia, to where a number of Chartists and workmen, movers of an Eight-Hours' Day in Britain, had emigrated and how the jingle

> Eight hours to work, eight hours to play,
> Eight hours to sleep, eight 'bob' a day,

is nothing but the threefold division of William of Malmesbury, (except for the reference to wages, which is a modern addition). There ought not to be the slightest doubt that there is an unbroken chain of ideas from 890 to 1890 regarding working hours. The Daily News wrote on March 6, 1899: "It should never be forgotten that Alfred was the inventor of the eight hour day." Let us substitute "the Alfredian tradition" for "Alfred", and it is certainly right.

*   *

*

Before concluding my book a few words may be said about working hours in the societies which had now and then been constructed by philosophers and social critics.

In general the planners had very little to say about working time. Plato's State, as is well-known, was a communist state in which the rich subsisted on the labour of the artisans and the farmers, who were allowed to have private property, as well as on the subjugated peoples and on the labour of the slaves. Indeed, slavery was the basis of society in Ancient Greece. The ruling class of the state did not work for themselves and the poor freemen lived on the dole. From the details given by Plato of his Utopian society it appears that his future state would be a Sovietdom or a Nazidom, — democracy was to be avoided. Plato says himself: "A commonwealth, however small it may be, consists indeed of two societies, one society for the rich and another for the poor, the one always fighting the other." Medieval social theories of an ideal society stressed the importance of a religious life, and although they contain many interesting and remarkable ideas, they cannot be characterized as social Utopias. In 1516 Thomas More's Utopia described a society which had abolished slavery, except for criminals, and which provided for state regulated copulation. In other respects the society was a communist régime. More thought it would be better without a king, since a bad king could ruin the state. He disliked wars immensely and decided that Utopia should be defended by mercenaries, — probably a detail from Antwerp, where he is said to have written his treatise. More attacked the idle rich, and idlers generally, and he calculated that if everybody worked in Utopia nobody need work more than six hours a day. This reduction of hours was much too drastic and impracticable to appeal to successive generations of Englishmen except in our own days. (See What's What in the Labor Movement: "Six hours day", — a very short entry.) More summed up his view on work in the fine words: "To love and to labour is the sum of living, and yet how manie think they live who neither labour nor love."

If More had suggested 6 hours a day for work, Campanella went one better in saying that 4 hours' work a day was enough. In the Civitas Solis (1600), which lacks the picturesque details so frequent in More's Utopia, he writes, "But in the City of the Sun all the public services, all the work done by the brain and the hands, are distributed evenly between all, so that the individual is scarcely (!) in need of more than four hours' work daily. The rest of his time he may spend in studies ... or in amusements." The cold character of his treatise has not hindered many later writers of the history of the future, such as Bellamy, Aldous Huxley, etc., from borrowing freely from him. Campanella was a disciple of Plato, for he lays down that work, diet, and copulation should be regulated by the state.

While More and Campanella belonged mentally to the Middle Ages in that they could never ignore the Church and its gospel, those who followed in their tracks were more mundane and critical. Montaigne does not discuss hours, nor does Bacon in New Atlantis, where Solomon's House or the college of the six days' work (i. e. an ordinary week) existed. The amusing introductory pages of Burton's Anatomy of Melancholy ("Democritus to the Reader") contain also the outlines of his private Utopia, where slavery was not tolerated, but no problem of working-time is discussed. And thus we can go on finding that there were no theories as regards working hours. The question was not so much time, as pay, in the various stages of English society. Harington's Oceana, Rousseau's Contrat Social, Spence's Crusonia or Spensonia, Marx's Capital (where "the normal day" does not fix definitely the hours), Samuel Butler's Erewhon (1872; a satire indicating a longing away from industrial society), and, later, Edward Bellamy's Looking Backward (1888), William Morris's News from Nowhere (1892; he is afraid that some day people will miss work), Jack London's The Iron Heel, do not enter upon a discussion of working hours. The only exceptions are Robert Owen's visions of a new society, for there different numbers of working hours (eventually 8) are advanced; and, quite recently, Aldous Huxley, whose Brave New World (Albatross Bks 1933) brings us some six hundreds of years forward, to a society founded on dictatorship and technical efficiency; the people of that time have their fill of sexual pleasure but all births are carefully produced in test-tubes. The question of working hours is easily solved (p. 223): "Seven and a half hours of mild, unexhausting labour" is the rule for eight ninths of the population. "They might ask for shorter hours. Technically, it would be perfectly simple to reduce all lower-caste working hours to three or four. But would they be any happier for that? No, they wouldn't ... The whole of Ireland was put on to the four-hour day (a century and a half ago). Unrest and a large increase in the consumption of *soma* (a kind of intoxicating pills); that was all. Those three and a half hours of extra leisure were so far from being a source of happiness, that people felt constrained to take a holiday from them. The Inventions Office is stuffed with plans for labour-saving processes. Thousands of them. (Mustapha Mond made a lavish gesture.) And why don't we put them into execution? For the sake of the labourers; it would be sheer cruelty to afflict them with excessive leisure."

Other modern visionary writers telling us of the future of mankind, or a certain country, such as Richard Jefferies's After London (1885); H. G. Wells's The Time Machine; Anatole France's L'Île des Pingouins; Carel Capek, the Czech dramatist, in R. U. R. (The Revolt of the Robots); Karin Boye, the Swedish authoress, in Kallocain; George Orwell in Nineteen eighty-four; and, in a way, Robert Graves in Seven Days in New Crete, have not thought fit to include any mention of working hours, and with reason. While the earlier writers looked forwards to the realization of a happy age, whatever its civilization and technique, modern writers are full of scepticism and despair. Technical civilization is striding hurriedly towards the perfection of scientific knowledge, including the experiences of human behaviour and motive, while the happiness of individuals, of private citizens, and even of the masses, is destroyed. All the optimism of past ages, the Victorian — and, earlier, Southey's, and even Thomas Burnet's of the 17 c.[30] — belief in progress, is gone.

---

[30] See ERNEST LEE TUVESON, Millennium and Utopia. A Study in the Background of the Idea of Progress. Univ. of California Press. Berkeley 1949.

BIBLIOGRAPHY

AELFRIC, Colloquies (in Stevenson, Early Scholastic Colloquies. Anecdota Oxon.) 1929.

AELFRIC, De Temporibus Anni. EETS orig. s. 213. 1942.

CHAUCER, G., The Poetical Works. From the Text of Professor Skeat. Vol. III. Oxf. Univ. Press.

COBBETT, W., Rural Rides. Nelson ed.

DISRAELI, Coningsby. Longmans, Green & Co. London n. d.

— Sybil or The Two Nations. Ed. London 1900.

— The Revolutionary Epick. Ed. 1864.

EETS orig. s. = Early English Text Society original series.

GASKELL, MRS., Mary Barton. Ed. 1947.

GOLDSMITH, OLIVER, She Stoops to Conquer. Tauchnitz ed.

LIEBERMANN, F., Die Gesetze der Angelsachsen. I Halle 1903. II: I Halle 1906. II: II Halle 1912.

LYTTON, LORD, Paul Clifford. Ed. 1896.

OWEN, ROBERT, A New View of Society and Other Writings. Ed. G. D. H. Cole. Everyman's Library.

— The Life of ... Ed. M. Beer. London 1920.

SCOTT, Rob Roy. Henry Frowde. Oxf. Univ. Pr. Oxford n. d.

— The Fair Maid of Perth. Oxf. Univ. Pr. Oxford 1911.

TAYLOR, JOHN, (the Water Poet), Early Prose and Poetical Works. Ed. London 1888.

*

ALFRED (= Samuel Kydd), The History of the Factory Movement. I. II. London 1857.

ASHTON, T. S., The Industrial Revolution 1760—1830. Home Univ. Library.

CAMP, CHARLES, The Artisan in Elizabethan Literature. Columbia Univ. Pr. 1924.

COLE, G. D. H., A Short History of the British Working Class Movement 1789—1937. London 1937.

— Attempts at General Union. London 1953.

CUNNINGHAM, W., The Growth of English Industry and Commerce during the Early and Middle Ages. Cambridge 1896.

DRIVER, CECIL, Tory Radical. The Life of Richard Oastler. Oxf. Univ. Pr. 1946.

GASKELL, P., Artisans and Machinery. London 1836.

GJÖRES, AXEL, Robert Owen. Stockholm 1932.

HALÉVY, ÉLIE, History of the English People. II. Pelican Bks.

HAMMOND, J. L. & BARBARA, (The) Town Labourer 1760—1832). London 1925.

— The Village Labourer 1760—1832. London 1924.

JARS, GABRIEL, Metallurgische Reisen … von Jahr 1757 bis 1769. Aus der Französischen übersetzt, hrsg. C. A. Gerhard. I. II. Berlin 1777. III. IV. Berlin 1785.

LUDLOW & LLOYD JONES, Die arbeitenden Klassen Englands in sozialer und politischer Beziehung. Berlin 1868.

MAC COBY, S., The Radical Tradition 1763—1914. London 1952.

MACCOBY, S., English Radicalism 1832—1852. London 1935.

MARX, KARL, Capital. Abridged and with an Introduction by John Strachey. Ed. Nelson.

Statutes of the Realm. I—II. London 1816.

STEFFEN, GUSTAF, Studien zur Geschichte des englischen Lohnarbeiters. I—III. Berlin 1900—05.

THOMAS, M. W., The Early Factory Legislation. Leigh-on-Sea. 1948.

THORPE, B., Ancient Laws and Institutions of England. 1840.

UNWIN, GEORGE, The Gilds & Companies of London. London 1938.

WADE, JOHN, History of the Middle and Working Classes. 3rd ed. London 1835.

WEBB, SIDNEY and BEATRICE, The History of Trade Unionism. London 1920.

WILSON, R. M., The Lost Literature of Medieval England. London 1952.

WRIGHT, C. E., The Cultivation of Saga in Anglo-Saxon England. Edinburgh 1939.

INDEX

Bennett, H. S. 53
Bentham, Jeremy 110, 131
Berkeley, Bishop 123
Bicknell, Alexander 68, 75
Bilfinger, G. 16, 21, 77
Birch, Thomas 61
Blackmore, Sir Richard 54
Blake, William 77, 100
Blue Monday 49
Boethius 17
Borde, Andrew 76
Boswell, James 80, 108
Bosworth-Toller 23
Boye, Karin 141
Bradshaw, Henry 37, 74
Brewer, J. S. 31
bright nights in Britain 10 f.
Broling, Gustaf 97 f.
Browne, Waldo R. 123
Buber, Martin 137
building operatives 38—43, 51, 99, 133
Burdett, Sir Francis 105
Burke, Edmund 69, 70, 75, 105
Burnet, Thomas 141
Burns, Robert 116
Burns, Rev. Thomas 131
Burt, Thomas 136
Burton, Robert 76, 140
Butler, Cuthbert 13, 14, 46
Butler, Samuel 140
Byrhtferth 12
Byron, Lord 104, 119

Calais ordinance 38, 41 ff., 45, 46, 47, 49, 51
Camden, William 57, 60
Camp, Charles 84
Campanella 140
Campbell, Thomas 108
Cannan, Edwin 88
Canute 24, 116
Capek, Carel 141
Capgrave, John 33, 34
Carney, Edward 5
Carte, Thomas 66, 75
casual combinations of workers 52
10*

Caxton, William 53 f., 55, 74
Chambers, R. W. 56
Chamberlayne, Edward 92
Charlemagne 18
Chartists 129, 130, 131, 132, 135
Chaucer, Geoffrey 7, 8, 12, 43, 54, 76
child labour 83, 84, 88, 97, 98, 99—102, 103, 106, 114 f., 124 f., 126 f.
Cistercians 9, 16
clepsydra 8
closing (h)ale 52
Cobbler's Monday 49, (95), 96
Cobbett, William 118, 126
Cobden, Richard 131
Coburn, K. 110
Coke, Sir Edward 80
Cole, G. D. H. 113, 118, 122, 126, 136
Coleridge, S. T. 110, 117
Colman & Garrick 95
Columbus, Samuel 78
Commelin, Jerome 56
Comenius 77 f., 137
Conybeare, J. W. 62
Cook, James, Captain 7
Cooper, Thomas 61
Coppée, François 138
Cottle, Joseph 55
Coulton, C. G. 53
Cowper, William 108, 116
Cox, Harold, see Webb
Coxe, H. O. 33, 34
Crabbe, George 100, 101
Crawford, S. J. 12
Croker, John Wilson 80
Cronqvist, Corfitz 134
Cunningham, Peter 119
Cunningham, W. 84, 85, 115
Cursor Mundi 29

Daniel, Samuel, 64, 74, 75
David, F. A. 73
dawn (»atte morne») 39, 40, 41, 44, 45, 46, 47, 82
daylight 39—52
day-work 48, 52
Defoe, Daniel 99, 116

serfdom (Anglo-Saxon) 22 ff., 25
seven and a half hour day 141
Shaftesbury, A. A. 105
Shakespeare 53, 63, 79, 86, 93, 94, 95
Sharpe, J. 61
Sheavyn, Ph. 77
Shelley 104, 117
Shrove Tuesday 95
Sidney, Sir Philip 117
Siegfried, André 132
Simeon, see Symeon of Durham
six hour day 102, 125, 139 f.
slavery 22 ff., 25, 104, 105, 108, 109,
    110, 136, 139
sleep 39, 40, 42, 44, 45, 46, 47, 48, 50,
    76, 82
Sloane, Sir John 81
slogans about working hours 113, 122,
    123, 128, 134, 138
slowing down 38, 39, 40, 41, 47, 51, 52
Smith, L. Toulmin 61
Smith, Adam 87, 88, 104 f.
social conditions 21—26, 52, 83, 84, 85,
    98—103, 104, 112, 125, 136
Society for National Regeneration 3,
    118, 126, 129
Southey, Robert 71, 101, 108, 110, 112,
    113, 117, 125, 141
Soviet Russia 104
Sparke, Joseph 60, 75
Spectator 94, 117
Speed, John 63, 74, 116
Spelman, Sir John 57—59, 60, 74, 75
Spence, Thomas 125, 140
Statute of Labourers 41
Statutes of the Realm 45, 46, 47, 48, 49,
    50, 52, 82, 83, 84, 85, 92, 96, 97, 99,
    100, 101, 102, 107, 110, 111, 115
Steele, Sir Richard 94
Steffen, Gustaf 48, 50, 51, 82, 115, 136,
    137
Stephens, Rev. J. R. 136
Stephens, James 132, 133
Sterne, Laurence 65
Stevenson, W. H. 18, 21, 26, 30, 32,
    33, 34, 56, 60

Stewart, Agnes M. 55
Stirling ordinance 82
Stone, Gilbert 62
Stonor Papers 52
Stow, John 56, 63, 74
Strathmore, Lord 92
Strutt, Joseph 68, 72, 75
Stubbs, Bishop 33
Sunday 22 ff., 50, 86, 98
sundial 8, 28
Sutcliffe, J. T. 133
Svedenstjerna, Erik 97
Sweet, Henry 56
Symeon of Durham 27, 32, 65
symmetry 29 f., 115
Sympson, Rev. J. 55
Sypher, Wylie 108

Tacitus 11
Tait, J. 118
Tawney, R. H. 49, 103
Taylor, John 7
ten hours a day 91, 92, 102
Ten Hour Day 117, 126, 127, 128, 129,
    137
Ten-Hour Philosophy 135
tending 38, 86, 87, 90, 91, 92
Thackeray, W. M. 82
Thomas, M. W. 4, 99, 100, 101, 102,
    103, 105, 111, 112, 126, 127, 130, 136
Thomas, P. G. 30
Thomson, James 54, 93, 116
Thorpe, B. 22, 27, 53
three eights, the 30, 113, 123, 138
threefold division of the 24 hours 3, 13,
    15, 16, 17, 27, 30, 31, 32, 34, 35, 36,
    37, 56, 57, 58, 59, 60, 61, 62, 63, 64,
    65, 66, 67, 68, 69, 73, 75, 76, 77, 113,
    115, 116, 122, 126, 138, 139
Thule 10 f.
time division, jingles about 10, 80, 81;
    measurers 3, 8, 18 ff., 21, 27, 30, 62,
    71, 73, 116; reckoning, primitive 3,
    6 f., 28; ancient 3, 8, 9, 13; Anglo-
    Saxon 9 ff.; monastic 13 ff., 16, 28,
    30; by the wheel-clock 3, 8, 16